# The Great Southern
# Wild Game Cookbook

# The Great Southern Wild Game Cookbook

## by Sam Goolsby

PELICAN PUBLISHING COMPANY

Gretna 1980

**Library of Congress Cataloging in Publication Data**

Goolsby, Sam.
  The great southern wild game cookbook.

  Includes index.
  1. Cookery (Game)   I. Title.
TX751.G56     641.6'91     79-27954
ISBN 0-88289-226-6

Manufactured in the United States of America

Published by Pelican Publishing Company, Inc.
1101 Monroe Street, Gretna, Louisiana 70053

Designed by Mike Burton

*To my late, beloved father: sportsman, raconteur, gourmet, and great all-round dad.*

# Contents

# *Foreword*

THE QUEST OF WILD GAME is my choice for a restful, heart-throbbing, fruitful, tiring, gainful, and exhilarating hobby. Preparing for and anticipating the kill can ease the pangs of mentally tiring and physically debilitating work. Plan now for this quest and use its fruits as memories of pleasure for months to come.

Game as you like it—that's what it's like at Cedar Creek Hunting Lodge. Hearty food for robust men with similar appetites is the order of every day during hunting season at Cedar Creek. After ten years of operating the lodge, it has become increasingly difficult for me to beg a little cut of the kill for camp meat. The first year was generally one of little enthusiasm by the hunters for venison to take home. Some would say, "It's the hunting for me; you can keep the meat." Others declared, "I'll take a hind quarter home for my brother-in-law, but my wife won't let me bring any deer meat into the house."

The next year the hunters said, "Keep the shoulders for some of that good stew; they're a little shot up anyway. Don't forget to flesh out that loin. My wife won't let me in the house without it." This year, everybody who comes brings an ice chest. Nobody will throw us a heart or a liver, whether it's shot up or not.

We have been told that the venison from this, the Piedmont area of Georgia, is the best anywhere. This could possibly be attributed to trace minerals or the general diet of the whitetail deer.

Any number of things are necessary to enhance the flavor of your meat. The first is choosing your buck. This requires a predetermined choice of table trophy over wall trophy, as the two are not always the same. Also, you must have a fast gun and a quick, appraising eye. I haven't met a hunter yet who would pass up a tough, stringy twelve point Boone and Crockett trophy for a chance at a tender, succulent spike buck. However, with the proper appreciation for its culinary qualities, no one will look at this young buck with disdain.

Proper field dressing is the second step to having a delightful meal of venison. And this is critical. This step is detailed in another section of the cookbook, as is the third step, meat cutting and handling.

This book is designed to offer everyone a chance at some of the food as prepared at Cedar Creek Hunting Lodge, Monticello, Georgia, although we'd rather have you hunting with us.

Boys, cook one meal a month like some of the following, and you've made a friend of the lady at home. Scan the following pages and treat yourself to the finest of game cookery.

# Acknowledgments

SO MANY GRATIFYING gifts of friendship are mine that mere words of thanks seem grossly inadequate. As my interest in game cooking progressed from one of casual pursuit to a consuming love, many intellectual and spiritual aids have come my way. I accept these as personal displays and will respond in kind.

As I view the world outdoors I perceive all living things creating or maintaining a viable balance of nature. I hold the philosophy that humans are an integral part of this balance and their sensible harvest of these animals includes their utilization for food and fur. I thank God for this arrangement and many fine sportspersons for helping me realize it.

To Alice Human I offer my thanks for her constant love and encouragement. She knows how to be a superb sister.

My thanks also go to: Dr. Everett Kuglar, whose gargantuan appetite for life and food makes it impossible for a fun-loving cook to fail. Also my thanks for his recipe for Game Pie from Williamsburg.

Frank Hatcher for his roast shank of venison. The inspiration for this dish is of dubious origin, but its quality is unsurpassed in my opinion.

Duke Rogero for "Duke's Wine Birds" (doves). Duke's birds are always tender as a mother's love because he has far less trouble getting his limit in the early season while the birds are not yet wary but very tender.

Juanita Hardee for her Spanish Rice and non-Hispanic Peach Ice Cream recipes.

Ernie Liner, the author of an excellent herpetological cookbook, with whom I have collaborated in science and cooking.

Dayton Malone, who owns an inimitable grasp for life and its other than material rewards. He has had a great influence on my understanding of coastal life and its gastronomical rewards.

My wife Shirley and children Zell, Ray, Sis, and Boo, the objects of my love and the testers of my many culinary experiments. My additional thanks to their gastrointestinal stamina.

# Appetizers

# Dill Dip

1 cup real mayonnaise
2 tsp. grated onion
½ tsp. dried dill weed
1 tsp. salt

1 cup sour cream
1 tsp. dry mustard
2 tsp. lemon juice

Combine all ingredients and chill. Can be served with chips, crackers, or your favorite raw vegetables. Makes 2 cups.

# South of the Border Dip

1 medium avocado, peeled and
  minced
2 tomatoes, peeled, seeded, and
  minced
1 small onion, peeled and minced
½ small green pepper, minced

dash of Tabasco sauce
½ tsp. Worcestershire sauce
½ tsp. salt
2 tbsp. lime juice
½ tsp. dry mustard

Combine all ingredients and blend until smooth. Yields 1 cup.

# Seashore Dip

1 7-oz. can minced clams
6 oz. cream cheese
1 tsp. lemon juice
dash of cayenne pepper

½ tsp. dried basil
3 sprigs parsley, stems removed
½ tsp. salt

Crumble cream cheese into blender. Add remaining ingredients, reserving liquid from clams. Blend well. If a softer mixture is desired, add small amount of liquid from clams. Yields 1 cup.

# Venison Liver Pâté

1 can (3- or 4-oz.) chopped
  mushrooms
1 envelope unflavored gelatin
1 10½-oz. can condensed beef
  bouillon
1 tsp. Worcestershire sauce

2 tbsp. brandy
½ cup pitted ripe olives
1 venison liver, boiled
½ cup pitted ripe olives
½ cup parsley leaves

Combine liquid from mushrooms with gelatin to soften. To this add ½ cup of boiling bouillon, in order to dissolve the gelatin. Add remaining ingredients and blend.

Pour into mold and chill until firm (approximately four hours or overnight). Unmold on chilled plate and garnish as desired. Makes 3 cups.

# Alcoholic Cheddar Dip

½ lb. mild cheddar cheese, cubed
1 7-oz. bottle of beer
1 tbsp. Worcestershire sauce

dash of cayenne pepper
½ tsp. dry mustard
2 oz. Gruyère cheese, cubed

Blend all ingredients, except cheddar cheese, until smooth. Add cheddar cheese cubes gradually and continue to blend until smooth. Yields 1½ cups.

# Braunschweiger Spread

¼ medium onion, chopped
½ lb. Braunschweiger, cubed
2 sprigs parsley

1 rib celery, chopped
2 tbsp. pickle juice
1 tsp. Tabasco sauce

Blend all ingredients until smooth. Makes 1½ cups.

# Egg and Avocado Dip

6 hard-cooked egg yolks
3 ripe avocados, peeled and
  chopped
dash of pepper
½ small onion, chopped

3 tbsp. cider vinegar
¾ tsp. chili powder
1½ tsp. salt
3 tbsp. parsley flakes

Blend all ingredients until smooth. Yields three cups.

# Bacon-Wrapped Oysters

1 pt. oysters, drained
smoked bacon

1 lemon
Worcestershire sauce

Cut bacon strips into thirds and wrap one around each oyster. Secure with toothpicks. Drop several drops each of lemon juice and Worcestershire sauce on oysters. Place over charcoal on a fine mesh grill or broil in oven until bacon is browned. Add some garlic cloves and a few hickory chips to the coals for added flavor.

For a great shrimp sauce, combine juice from oysters, 1 stick butter, and a few drops of Worcestershire.

Serves eight.

# Barbecue Frank Slices

1 package franks
barbecue sauce of choice

Cut franks into bite-sized pieces. Place in saucepan with barbecue sauce. Cook until franks are done. Serve in hot chafing dish with toothpicks to spear franks. Serves four to six.

# Nuts and Bolts

1 6-oz. package pretzel sticks
1 lb. mixed nuts
1 package Cheerios
1 package Rice Chex
1 package Wheat Chex

1½ cups butter or salad oil
2 tbsp. Worcestershire sauce
1 tbsp. garlic salt
1 tbsp. onion salt
1 tbsp. celery salt

Melt butter or oil in a large roasting pan. Add cereals, nuts, and pretzels. Combine last four ingredients and add to roasting pan. Cook covered in a 225-degree oven for 30 minutes. Uncover and cook until brown and crisp, stirring often. Cool, put in quart jars, and keep closed until needed.

# Venison Appetizer Meatballs

1 lb. ground venison
¼ cup milk
1 medium onion, minced
¾ tsp. salt
½ cup soft bread crumbs
1 cup flour

3 tbsp. butter
¼ tsp. thyme
3 tbsp. molasses
3 tbsp. vinegar
3 tbsp. prepared mustard
¼ cup ketchup

Combine first five ingredients, shape into bite-sized meatballs, and flour lightly. In skillet, melt butter and brown meatballs. Remove meatballs, combine remaining ingredients, and stir into skillet. Bring to a boil, add meatballs, and simmer 10 minutes, stirring occasionally.

# Chicken Livers with Bouillon Sauce

smoked bacon
desired amount of livers
1 tsp. salt
2 chicken bouillon cubes

½ stick butter or margarine
juice of 1 lemon
2 cloves garlic, crushed
1 tbsp. brown sugar

Dissolve bouillon cubes in melted butter or margarine. Add all other ingredients except bacon and livers.

Wrap chicken livers with one-third strip of bacon, securing with toothpicks. Add several drops of the first mixture to each liver and grill or broil until bacon is browned. Baste occasionally.

# Olive and Beef Wraps

smoked bacon
1 package dried beef

1 jar ripe olives
cheese of your choice

Stuff olives with cheese and wrap in dried beef and bacon. Grill or broil until bacon is browned.

# Marinated Smoked Shrimp

raw shrimp, unshelled
1 clove garlic, crushed
1 medium bottle Italian dressing

Marinate shrimp 1 hour in Italian dressing and garlic. Smoke shrimp on slow grill containing hickory chips for 1 hour.

# Shrimp and Olive Deviled Eggs

6 large boiled eggs
¼ cup mayonnaise
½ tsp. dry mustard
baby shrimp
sliced green olives

2 tsp. stuffed olives,
    finely chopped
8 medium boiled shrimp,
    finely chopped

Split eggs lengthwise. Mix mayonnaise, mustard, chopped olives, and shrimp with the egg yolks. Stuff egg whites with this mixture. Garnish with baby shrimp and green olive slices. Serves six.

# Soups

# Curried Pea Soup

1½ cups cooked peas
1 chicken bouillon cube
1½ tsp. curry powder
½ cup milk

1 tbsp. flour
2 tbsp. butter
2½ cups chicken broth
salt to taste

Blend the first four ingredients until smooth. Combine with the last four ingredients. Pour the mixture into a saucepan and simmer until thick, stirring occasionally. Yields eight servings.

# Borscht

1 cup diced beets, cooked
pulp of ½ small lemon
1¾ cups sour cream

¼ tsp. onion salt
¼ tsp. salt
¼ tsp. celery salt

Blend all ingredients until smooth. Serve cold, garnished with sour cream if desired.

# Tuna Bisque

1 10½-oz. can condensed
   cream of asparagus soup
1 10½-oz. can condensed
   cream of mushroom soup

2½ cups milk
1 7-oz. can flaked tuna, drained
5 tbsp. sherry

Blend sherry, soups, and 1 cup milk until smooth. Add tuna and remaining milk. Pour into saucepan and simmer 10 minutes. Serves six.

# Vegetable Soup

1 smoked ham hock
2 qts. water
1 large onion, chopped
1 cup fresh corn
1 qt. peeled tomatoes

1 cup butter beans
3 medium potatoes, diced
1 cup sliced okra
salt and pepper to taste

Simmer ham hock in water for 2 hours. Add next four ingredients and cook 1 hour. Add okra and potatoes and simmer on low heat until tender. Salt and pepper to taste.

# Cedar Creek Seafood Chowder

4 cups cooked crabmeat
1 lb. shrimp, boiled and peeled
½ tsp. cayenne
½ tsp. celery salt
1 cup minced parsley

salt and pepper to taste
20 saltine crackers, pounded
½ stick butter
1 qt. cream

Sauté crabmeat and shrimp in small amount of butter for 5 minutes. Add remaining ingredients and simmer 30 minutes. Serve with boiled rice. Serves four.

# Okra Soup

1 lb. venison
3 lbs. fresh minced okra
10 tomatoes, peeled and chopped

dash each of salt, celery salt, pepper, and garlic salt

Simmer venison in 1 quart of water for 1 hour. Skim off foam and add all ingredients. Simmer again for 1 hour. Serve with rice. Serves four.

# Gazpacho

1 clove garlic, pressed
6 tomatoes, peeled and chopped
1 tbsp. paprika
½ cup red wine
½ lb. onions, peeled and chopped
2½ tbsp. olive oil

2 black olives, pitted and sliced
1 cucumber, peeled and thinly
  sliced
croutons
finely chopped parsley

Combine the first six ingredients and blend until smooth. Place in a saucepan and simmer 10 minutes. Add cucumbers and olives. Salt and pepper to taste. Soup may be sprinkled with parsley and garnished with croutons. Six servings.

# Creole Gumbo

1 stick butter
2 tbsp. flour
4 onions, minced
2 qts. hot stock
½ cup minced celery
1 clove garlic, minced
1 doz. raw oysters

3 bay leaves
1 cup minced green peppers
4 tsp. assorted spices (salt,
  pepper, thyme, and rosemary)
1 lb. shrimp, boiled and peeled
2 cups cooked crabmeat

Sauté onions in butter. Add flour and brown slowly. Pour in hot stock and all ingredients except shellfish. Add shrimp and simmer about 20 minutes, stirring occasionally. Add crabmeat and oysters, simmering until oysters curl. (Any fowl or game may be used in place of the shellfish.) Serves four.

# Chicken Gumbo

2 stalks celery, diced
1 medium onion, diced
1 small green pepper, diced
2 tbsp. bacon fat
1 cup cooked or canned okra
2 cups canned tomatoes
1⅓ cups uncooked rice

1 qt. turkey or chicken stock
1 tsp. salt
dash of pepper
2 cups cooked turkey or chicken, diced
2 tbsp. chopped parsley

Lightly sauté the first three ingredients in fat. Add the next six ingredients and bring to a boil. Lower heat and simmer 45 minutes. Add diced meat, heat, and serve with parsley. Makes four to six servings.

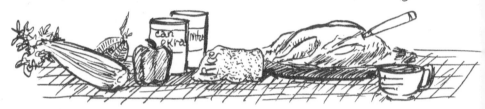

# Tomato Soup

1 large onion, minced
salt and pepper to taste
¼ lb. butter or margarine
2 tbsp. olive oil
½ tsp. dried basil
½ tsp. dried thyme

3 tbsp. tomato paste
2½ lbs. tomatoes
3¾ cups chicken broth
¼ cup flour
1 cup heavy cream
1 tsp. sugar

Combine salt, pepper, butter, olive oil, basil, and thyme. Sauté onions in this mixture. Add tomato paste and tomatoes. Cook 10 minutes.

Mix flour with a small amount of broth and add to tomato mixture. Add remaining broth and cook 20 minutes. Using part of the mixture at a time, blend in a blender until smooth. Return to saucepan and add cream and sugar. Heat and serve. Yields eight servings.

# Split Pea Soup

2 cups dried split peas
1 carrot, diced
1 onion, diced
2 stalks celery, diced
1 ham bone
¼ bay leaf

2 tbsp. butter or margarine
3 cups milk
dash of pepper
1 tsp. salt
chopped parsley

Prepare peas for cooking as directed on the package. Combine peas with next five ingredients and two quarts of water in a saucepan. Bring to a boil and simmer until peas are tender (about two hours). Cool slightly, remove ham bone, and using part of the mixture at a time, blend in a blender until smooth.

Return to saucepan and add next four ingredients. Heat, but do not boil. Sprinkle with parsley before serving. Serves eight.

# Salads and
# Salad Dressings

I WISH I KNEW how many times I wanted to get up and leave a restaurant after being served the salad. Soft, wet lettuce and a smudge of prepared dressing. Ugh!!!

Each course has a purpose. The salad sets the tone of the meal and places within your power the ability to make the meal a success.

An ample wooden bowl and a wooden fork and spoon (all rubbed with a garlic pod and salt) is the first step in making a salad a memorable thing. Escarole, lettuce, watercress, romaine, and endive can be used to complement many things. Make sure the leaves are dried fully to allow them to absorb your dressing. Leaves should be torn with fingers, never cut.

Wipe bowl clean with a moist cloth. Never work with soap and water, as this destroys the pleasant flavors that are now a part of your future salads.

## Sam's Sensational Wilted Slaw

8 strips smoked bacon  
½ head firm cabbage  
1 medium onion  
1 bell pepper  

½ cup vinegar  
¼ cup water  
½ tbsp. sugar  
salt to taste  

Fry and drain bacon, saving half the fat in the frying pan. Shred cabbage, onion, and pepper very finely and mix with crumbled bacon; salt lightly. Dissolve sugar in vinegar and water. Place the fat in the frying pan over heat; when hot, pour the vinegar mixture in while gently stirring. Pour over greens, toss, and serve immediately.

## Tossed Spinach Salad

Prepare in the same manner as Sam's Sensational Wilted Slaw but substitute torn, green spinach leaves and spring onions for greens. Garnish with sliced boiled eggs.

# Caesar Salad Supreme

### DRESSING

½ cup salad oil
1½ tsp. salt
¾ tsp. pepper
2 tsp. Worcestershire sauce

1 clove garlic, quartered
1 tsp. dry mustard
3 tbsp. vinegar
½ tsp. sugar

Combine all ingredients in a jar with a tight fitting lid. Shake well and refrigerate for at least one night.

### SALAD

½ green pepper, cut in thin strips
½ head endive
1 bunch watercress
2 cups croutons, buttered and
    toasted
1 cup grated Parmesan cheese
1 can anchovy fillets

½ cucumber
1 small head lettuce
1 egg, raw
6 radishes, sliced
1 cup (5 oz.) crumbled blue
    cheese

At serving time, combine well-chilled greens in a large bowl. Strain garlic from salad dressing and add to greens with cheese and croutons. Drop in the egg and toss until well mixed. Garnish with anchovy fillets and serve immediately. Serves eight.

# Avocado Dressing

1 avocado, grated or finely
    minced
½ cup orange juice

2 tsp. mayonnaise
pulp of ½ lemon
¼ tsp. salt

Blend all ingredients until smooth. Makes 1¼ cups of dressing.

# Bean Salad

1 can green beans
1 cup sliced celery
1½ cups sugar
1 can kidney beans
2 onions, sliced
1 cup vinegar
1 raw egg

1 can green limas
1 small jar pimentoes
1 can wax beans
1 green pepper, diced
½ cup salad oil
salt and pepper

Drain all beans and toss with the other vegetables and the egg in an adequately sized bowl. Heat oil, vinegar, and sugar; salt and pepper to taste. Allow mixture to cool slightly, pour over beans, and cool thoroughly before serving. Salad may be left in refrigerator to improve flavor.

# Garlic Dressing

2 cloves garlic, crushed
¼ tsp. white pepper
1 tsp. salt
½ tsp. paprika

¼ cup lemon juice
⅔ cup light cream
½ tsp. sugar
¾ cup salad oil

Blend all ingredients until smooth. Yields 2 cups.

# Blue Cheese or Roquefort Dressing

½ cup crumbled blue or
   Roquefort cheese
dash garlic powder
1 cup evaporated milk, undiluted

½ cup salad oil
¼ cup vinegar
½ tsp. salt

Blend all ingredients until smooth. Yields 2 cups.

# Old-Fashioned Salad Dressing

2 large eggs
⅔ cup cider vinegar
1 tsp. powdered onion
4 tsp. flour
1 tbsp. softened butter

4 tbsp. sugar
1 tsp. salt
salt and pepper to taste
1 cup light cream
3 tsp. dry mustard

Blend and allow to stand in refrigerator.

# Grapefruit Remoulade Dressing

¼ tsp. Tabasco
1 hard boiled egg, chopped
2 tbsp. frozen Florida grapefruit
  juice concentrate

½ cup mayonnaise
¼ cup chili sauce
2 tsp. horseradish

Blend Tabasco into mayonnaise. Reserve some of the chopped egg for garnish; combine the remaining egg and other ingredients and blend thoroughly. Makes 1 cup of dressing.

# Southern Potato and Cucumber Salad

4 large boiling potatoes, peeled
  and sliced
2 cucumbers, peeled and sliced
½ cup vinegar
½ tsp. sugar

8 strips smoked bacon
1 onion, thinly sliced
¼ cup water
salt to taste

Boil potatoes until done and drain. Fry bacon and reserve half of the drippings. Drain and crumble bacon into potatoes along with cucumbers and onions. Pour mixture of vinegar, water, and sugar into the hot fat. Pour over the salad, mix, and serve immediately.

# Cedar Creek Marinated Vegetables

2 large cauliflowers
1 bag carrots
1 bunch celery
8 cloves garlic
2 cans black olives
2 cans mushroom buttons

juice of 4 lemons (retain 2 halves
    for marinade)
2 large bottles Italian dressing
1 tbsp. garlic powder
salt to taste

Cut off cauliflower buds and split to bite size. Split carrots and celery into fourths, lengthwise, then cut pieces 2 inches long. Add drained mushrooms, olives, and garlic cloves. Sprinkle garlic powder over cut vegetables. Add lemon juice, lemon halves, and Italian dressing. Stir and refrigerate for 1 hour.

Remove from refrigerator, stir, and salt. Marinate for at least 2 hours more, stirring occasionally.

Serve in a large bowl. Use toothpicks to spear the morsels.

# German Potato Salad

6 potatoes, boiled, peeled, and
    diced
1 onion, diced
½ lb. bacon
1 tbsp. flour

1 tbsp. sugar
1 tsp. salt
½ tsp. pepper
½ cup vinegar
1 tsp. Angostura bitters

Fry bacon until brown and remove; sauté onion in fat. Add flour. Combine the next four ingredients with ½ cup water and add this gradually to the flour mixture in the pan. Add bitters and cook until smooth and glossy. Add potatoes and crumbled bacon and heat thoroughly. Serve warm to six diners.

# Cookout Salad Bowl

½ cup salad oil
¼ cup wine vinegar
½ tsp. Worcestershire
1 small onion, grated
¼ cup blue cheese

4 slices smoked bacon
¼ cup ketchup
½ tsp. salt
2 whole cloves
1 head lettuce

Mix everything but lettuce, cheese, and bacon; heat and stir. Chill the mixture after removing the cloves. Tear lettuce into bite-sized pieces in a garlic-rubbed salad bowl. Crumble bacon and cheese over the greens and toss, using some of the dressing.

Meats

Meats

VENISON TAKES A BACK SEAT to no other meat. Choose the proper animal during the hunt, field dress, cut, and cure it properly, and the only remaining factor for superb eating is the cooking. Along with the meat of elk, caribou, antelope, and other western and northern large game, which is very similar to deer meat and is prepared in an identical manner, venison is noted for its tremendous culinary quality. The fact that these meats are rarely served can be traced to two major reasons: difficult accessibility and difficult preparation.

Venison is a very lean meat that requires fat in its preparation. In contrast to good beef, there is no marbling in deer meat; no fat is veined throughout the venison. A larding needle is a valuable kitchen aid used to replace the inherent fat that nature has omitted, allowing these great animals to travel at high speeds for long distances.

Contrary to a popular belief, there is no need to soak venison in oils, wines, or vinegar to kill the wild taste. With proper preparation in the field, butcher shop, and kitchen, this soaking is not necessary. However, individual tastes dictate the value of marinade. I always maintain in my cooking an awareness of individual tastes, and would never discriminate against someone whose idea of "goodness" differed from mine. If possible I attempt to eliminate the potentially distasteful factor from every dish.

Remember, don't undercook venison. Generally, rare venison is not desirable, although I have enjoyed some prepared especially well. Usually rare venison is served as a whole ham or shoulder that has been injected with an oily, tart sauce by a meat syringe.

## *Venison Barbecue*

This is your chance to impress your friends with your culinary skills. I find this an excellent time to sit around and discuss many provocative subjects, while enjoying a cool beer, absorbing smoke, and occasionally poking the coals and basting the meat.

For opening day, we like to take an "archer killed yearling" (as the bow season is the month prior to the firearm season, usually October), properly cured and laid open flat on the grill wire. The carcass can be laid open by sawing through the bones on one side, lateral to the mid-line of spine and pelvis on the ventral side or the inside.

Build yourself a fire of oak and hickory, from which you'll remove coals for the cooking. You can use bricks or concrete blocks for your makeshift barbecue pit. Place a greased wire grill on blocks about 6 to 8 inches above a good bed of hot coals and lay your deer, "cut side" down to seal in any juices. Make a small mop by wrapping a clean, absorbent, non-raveling rag around the tip of a 3-foot-long rigid stick and tying it securely. Dip mop into cooking oil and baste well on the "up" side. Cook underside until well browned, turn, and mop this side with oil. Redistribute coals to add more heat to the hams and shoulders.

Cook slowly until about 30 minutes before completely done. Now replace the oil with your favorite barbecue sauce and mop frequently.

The front half may now be removed from the grill to be boned and finely chopped, as the hind half is thicker and requires more cooking. When done, the hind half is boned and chopped and mixed well with the other venison and barbecue sauce. Serve this to the thirty-odd people who have been anxiously awaiting the fruits of your oft-discussed hunting trip.

NOTE: I prefer to cook a pork shoulder along with the deer to be chopped and mixed with the venison.

## Frank's Roast Shank of Venison

MARINADE
1 part red wine
1 part oil
2 tbsp. soy sauce

| | |
|---|---|
| 1 venison ham | onion powder |
| ½ lb. bacon | 2 tbsp. Worcestershire |
| 2 large onions, sliced | garlic powder |
| 2 green peppers, sliced round | salt and pepper |
| 1 cup prepared mustard | 8 beef bouillon cubes |
| ½ lb. brown sugar | |

Marinate venison 2 to 3 hours. Rub garlic powder, onion powder, salt, and pepper on meat. Place ham on rack in Dutch oven. Cover the entire ham with bacon slices and lay on the sliced onions and peppers. Combine sugar, mustard, and Worcestershire sauce and pour over the vegetables. Add 4 cups water and 8 beef bouillon cubes to bottom of pan. (Be prepared to add more water.) Cover and cook at 300° for approximately 4 hours, basting often. You will be pleased. It's outstanding.

## Country Fried Venison

venison round steaks (1 medium
   steak per person)
garlic salt

flour
meat tenderizer
vegetable oil

Lay out venison and sprinkle meat tenderizer and garlic salt on each side. Tenderize thoroughly by pounding, dredge with flour, and fry in a liberal amount of fat (venison will soak up the fat so be prepared to add more). Pour off all but 2 tablespoons of fat.

Brown 2 tablespoons of flour over low heat. Add 1 cup water while stirring. Add milk and let simmer until thick and creamy. Place cooked meat in gravy and simmer for 10 minutes. Serve with rice.

TIP: Fat and bone marrow make venison stronger in taste, so it is advisable to remove these before freezing.

## Roast Shoulder of Flat Roast

Season roast with salt and pepper and cover entirely with bacon strips. Roast, uncovered, adding no water, in a 300- to 350-degree oven. Allow 20 to 25 minutes per pound. Your favorite sauce or gravy may be added when done.

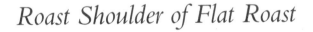

# Venison Burgers 1

2 lbs. ground venison
1 small onion, minced
2 tbsp. soy sauce or
   Worcestershire

1 clove of garlic, minced
⅔ cup dry red wine
4 tbsp. parsley, chopped
salt and pepper to taste

Combine ingredients, form into patties, and cook on grill or broil until done. Serve on hot buns with all the trimmings. Serves eight.

TIP: Add 2 pounds of pork to every 6 pounds of venison before grinding into hamburger. Pork or beef fat may be used—½ pound per 6 pounds venison.

# Venison Burgers 2

2 lbs. ground venison
2 eggs, beaten
⅛ tsp. pepper
½ lb. mild sausage or ground
   pork

1 medium onion, chopped
¼ tsp. marjoram
2 tbsp. melted fat
¼ tsp. monosodium glutamate
   (optional)

Mix venison, pork, and onion. Add other ingredients, form into patties, and brown in fat. Cover, reduce heat, and simmer about 10 minutes. Serves six.

# Sausage

Combine ¼ pound pork with 2 pounds venison, and grind with meat grinder. The sausage can then be seasoned with cayenne pepper, black pepper, sage, and salt, and rolled, and wrapped for the freezer. It may be wrapped in cheesecloth for smoking.

# Marinated Fillets

boneless venison loin
4 cloves pressed garlic
1 tbsp. soy sauce

1 cup cooking oil
2 tbsp. red wine
bacon strips

Cut loin in ¾-inch to 1-inch steaks. Bacon wrap and place in pan. Make a marinade of the other four ingredients, pour over fillets, and allow to stand for 1½ hours. Pan fry, broil, or grill over hickory chips.

TIP: Loins should be roasted, grilled or broiled. Less tender cuts are best when cooked with a moist heat, pot roasted, fried, ground for hamburgers, braised, or stewed.

# Braised Heart and Gravy

(1 heart for 2 people, 2 hearts for 4 people, and so on up to the Chinese population)

venison heart
flour
salt and pepper to taste
gravy (salt and pepper to taste)

2 tbsp. flour
1 cup milk
2 cups water

Cut open heart, removing sinew and large blood vessels. Slice across grain in strips about ½ inch thick. Salt and pepper strips and dredge in flour. Brown lightly on both sides in hot fat. Add 1 cup water, cover tightly, and simmer very slowly until tender (at least 2 hours).

For gravy, leave small amount of grease in pan with brown bits of flour from heart. Brown about 2 tablespoons of flour in pan and add a mixture of 1 cup milk and 2 cups water. Stir frequently and serve with heart. More or less liquid may be used, depending on the thickness of gravy desired. Sautéed onions, green peppers, and mushrooms are very good when added to gravy.

# Venison Pot Roast with Vegetables

3 to 4 lbs. venison roast
2 tbsp. butter
¼ cup cubed smoked bacon
1½ cups hot water
1 tbsp. fresh parsley, chopped
1 cup apple juice
1 tsp. salt
¼ tsp. thyme

¼ tsp. pepper
1 stalk celery, sliced diagonally
6 potatoes, peeled
6 carrots, peeled
6 onions, speared from side with
    toothpicks to hold them
    together

Insert cubes of smoked bacon into small cuts in roast. Brown meat in melted butter in deep casserole or Dutch oven. Add next six ingredients, cover, and simmer for 3 hours on top of stove or in oven at 325° until meat is tender.

Add vegetables about 1 hour before meal is to be served and cook until tender. Additional water may be added during cooking time if necessary. Remove meat and vegetables to platter and thicken liquid with 2 or 3 tablespoons browned flour or cornstarch. Serves six to eight.

# Venison Gravy

1 small onion, chopped
2 tbsp. flour
¼ cup bacon drippings
hot water

1 to 2 beef bouillon cubes
    (optional)
¼ cup red wine (optional)

Sauté onion in pan used to cook venison. Add bacon fat, then flour. Pour in enough hot water to make desired thickness. Beef cubes may be used; wine may also be added before serving.

# Suburban Venison Stew

3 to 4 lbs. venison shoulder or
  neck meat
3 tbsp. bacon drippings
¼ cup flour
1½ tsp. salt
½ tsp. pepper
1½ cups red wine

1 tsp. dried parsley
⅓ tsp. each basil, thyme,
  marjoram
2 cups hot water
6 potatoes, peeled and quartered
6 carrots, peeled and quartered
8 small onions

Trim meat of sinews, bones and excess fat, cut into cubes, dredge in flour, and brown in bacon drippings (in deep pan). Add all of the rest of the ingredients, except the vegetables, cover, and bring mixture to a boil. Reduce heat and simmer 2 hours.

Add potatoes and carrots, cover, and simmer 30 minutes. Add onions and simmer ½ to 1 hour longer until vegetables are tender. Serve hot with biscuits. Serves eight.

# Venison Meatballs

1½ lbs. ground venison
3 slices soft bread
¼ cup water
1 medium chopped onion
¼ cup butter

¾ cup milk
1 tbsp. flour
2 tsp. salt
¼ tsp. pepper

Soak bread in water a few minutes, then break into pieces, pressing out water. Combine bread with venison, onion, salt, and pepper. Form into meatballs, chill 20 minutes, then brown in butter. Cover and simmer 15 minutes.

Remove meatballs and combine flour, milk, salt, and pepper to taste in pan to make gravy. (Brown flour first.)

Serves four.

# Broiled Venison Steaks

*4 venison steaks, 1½ in. thick*
*salt and pepper to taste*

Preheat broiler. Place steaks on broiler rack about 3 inches below heat. Leave broiler door open. Broil 7 to 10 minutes, season, turn over, and broil about 6 minutes, or until done. Serves four.

# Cedar Creek Venison Meat Loaf

*2 lbs. ground venison*
*½ lb. pork or sausage*
*1 tsp. salt*
*½ cup onion, minced*
*1 egg, beaten*
*¼ cup celery, chopped*

*1 cup soft bread crumbs*
*dash pepper*
*¼ cup parsley, chopped*
*1 cup milk (1 cup tomatoes may*
*be used instead)*

Combine all ingredients and mold into a loaf. Line pan with foil and cook meat loaf uncovered in a 350-degree oven for about 2 hours or until done. Serves eight to ten.

# Hunter's Style Venison

*3 lbs. venison, cubed*
*2 tbsp. butter*
*salt and pepper to taste*
*2 sprigs crushed thyme*
*1 minced onion*
*1 clove minced garlic*
*2 bay leaves*

*1 qt. beef consommé*
*1 tbsp. flour*
*½ lb. fresh chopped mushrooms*
*2 cups warm water*
*1 lemon peel, grated*
*1 inch cube ham, minced*

Salt and pepper venison and brown in melted butter. Add onion and sauté. Next add thyme, garlic, bay leaves, and ham; simmer about 2 to 3 minutes. Add flour and cook about 5 minutes.

Add water, letting mixture cool to a simmer, then add beef consommé and cook slowly 1 hour. Add lemon peel and mushrooms and cook 30 minutes. More seasoning may be added. Serves eight.

## Hunter's Liver

Liver is usually prepared by frying and is best cooked as soon as possible after the deer is killed. Cut liver into ¼-inch slices, salt and pepper to taste, dredge with flour, and fry in very hot, clean vegetable oil. If cooked too long, the liver loses its flavor and becomes tough.

Onions served with liver should be cooked separately. Liver may also be served with a slice of bacon on each prepared slice.

## Glorious Liver

*1 lb. venison liver, cut in ½-in.*
  *strips*
*paprika*
*flour*
*salt and pepper*
*2 tbsp. salad oil*

*2 tbsp. butter*
*1 clove garlic, minced*
*2 tbsp. snipped parsley*
*½ cup dry white wine*
*¾ cup sour cream*

Batter liver in mixture of flour, paprika, salt, and pepper, and cook in pan with heated oil and butter. Season liver with minced garlic as it is cooking. Remove liver to hot plate and pour off most of fat in pan.

Add parsley and wine, cooking so that browned bits from bottom of pan are brought up. Add sour cream and heat, but do not boil. Add liver strips and heat. Serve over rice or buttered noodles. Yields four servings.

# Venison Chili Con Carne

1 can kidney beans
1 large onion, chopped
1 green pepper, chopped
1 lb. ground venison and pork
1 large can tomato sauce
1½ tbsp. salt
1 tsp. Worcestershire sauce
1 tbsp. ketchup

2 tbsp. brown sugar
dash of paprika
dash of cayenne pepper
3 whole cloves
1 bay leaf
2 tbsp. chili powder
1 cup water

Brown onion, pepper, and meat in 2 tablespoons bacon drippings. Add tomato sauce, water, and seasonings. Simmer 15 minutes and taste to your satisfaction. Add beans and simmer for 3 hours. Approximately four servings.

# Venison Mincemeat

4 lbs venison
3 lbs. apples, peeled and
    quartered
¾ lb. beef suet
2 qts. cider
2 lbs. seedless raisins
12 oz. currants

1 tsp. allspice
1 tsp. salt
1 tbsp. ground ginger
1 tbsp. nutmeg
1 tbsp. cinnamon
1 tbsp. ground cloves

Trim fat from venison and cook slowly in water until tender. Refrigerate venison in liquid overnight. In the morning skim fat off liquid and grind venison. Grind apples and suet.

Blend all ingredients in a large pot and simmer 2 hours. Use 2 parts mincemeat to 1 part chopped apples for pies.

# Venison Jerky

Cut lean meat into strips less than ½ inch wide. String these on a wire and dip in a pot of boiling salted water (1 cup salt to a gallon water). When meat loses red color, lift from water and drain. Pepper and spices may now be added according to taste and meat is ready to dry (usually 2 to 4 days).

During drying process, meat should be covered at night and protected from rain. A smudge fire of non-resinous wood will keep insects away, but it must not overheat the meat. Pepper may also be added to help keep flies away. Meat is sometimes hung in screened buildings to cure, but this takes more time.

# Creole Liver

| | |
|---|---|
| 1 lb. venison liver, thinly sliced | 3 slices bacon |
| 2 tbsp. flour | 1 medium onion, thinly sliced |
| salt and pepper to taste | 1 cup vegetable juice cocktail |

Brown bacon, drain, and set aside. Dredge liver slices in mixture of flour, salt, and pepper, and brown in small amount of bacon fat. Add onion, vegetable juice cocktail, and crumbled bacon. Simmer, covered, for 10 minutes or until liver is tender. Makes four servings.

# Venison Cordon Bleu

Take four small, ¼-inch thick steaks and pound them very well. Sprinkle with garlic powder and a very small amount of oregano. On top of one steak place a slice of Swiss cheese, a pinch of chopped or dried parsley, and 1 teaspoon of red wine. Place over this another of the pounded steaks and pinch the edges together. Spear the edges with four toothpicks and pan fry in butter until done.

# Venison Tacos

1½ lbs. ground venison and pork
1 can green chilis, chopped
2 tbsp. flour
12 tortillas

2 cups grated cheese
2 tbsp. butter
2 cups tomato juice
lettuce and onions, chopped

Sauté chilis, meat, and onions in butter; add flour and tomato juice. Simmer until thick. Bake the packaged tortillas and serve so that each person can spoon in the meat mixture and top with chopped lettuce, onions, and grated cheese. Serves four hungry people.

# Venison Sauerbraten

2 lbs. venison chuck, round, or
   rump roast
water to cover
3 bay leaves
1 cup vinegar
5 whole cloves
6 peppercorns

1 cup celery, sliced
6 carrots
6 onions
10 crushed gingersnaps
1 tbsp. sugar
3 tbsp. fat

Place venison in covered dish after removing all fat. Combine vinegar, bay leaves, cloves, and peppercorns and pour over meat. Cover with water and refrigerate, covered, for at least 5 days.

Remove meat and reserve liquid for gravy. Brown meat in fat and add vegetables and 2 cups of reserved marinade. Simmer until tender (about 1½ hours).

Remove meat and vegetables and add gingersnaps and sugar to remaining liquid to make gravy. Serves four or five.

# Danish Roast Venison
## (Stegt Dyrekolle)

1 leg venison
6 oz. pork fat strips, 2 in. long by
   ⅓ in. wide
2 tbsp. olive oil
1½ tsp. salt
¼ tsp. pepper
1 cup melted butter
½ tbsp. ground ginger

4 cups meat stock
2 tbsp. orange marmalade
⅓ cup flour
¼ tbsp. grated orange rind
2 tbsp. butter
5 tsp. Chianti wine
1 cup dry sherry

Wipe venison, dry well, and remove sinews, skin, and membranes. Roll pork strips in salt, pepper, and ginger. Insert fat into venison at regular intervals, allowing fat to show at both ends. Rub roast with oil, place in roasting pan, pour melted butter over venison, and bake at 325° for 4 to 5 hours or until meat is tender and brown. Baste with mixture of ½ cup sherry and meat stock every 15 minutes during baking. When done, remove venison from pan and fat from natural gravy. Combine butter and flour, making a smooth paste. Add orange rind and wine (or vinegar) and stir into the gravy in the pan. Cook 10 minutes, add rest of sherry and orange marmalade and baste roast with the gravy ½ to 1 hour in slow oven. Serves twelve.

# Liver Bordelaise

1 deer liver
½ cup red wine
1 cup onions, minced

1 clove garlic, pressed
½ stick butter

Slice the liver into ⅓-inch slices and dust with flour. Brown well in oil. Add remaining ingredients and stew for 1 hour or until done. Venison liver may be eaten immediately after the deer is dressed. Serves six.

# Cherokee Indian Poyha
## (Meat loaf)

1 lb. ground venison
½ cup cornmeal
1 tsp. salt
1 small onion, chopped

½ cup water
1 can whole kernel corn
2 eggs

Mix cornmeal and water in bowl and let stand. Brown venison in hot fat and when done add corn and onion. Cook 10 minutes. Add cornmeal and water mixture, eggs, and salt. Cook 15 minutes. Place in greased loaf pan and bake at 350° for 30 to 45 minutes.

# Sweet-and-Sour Venison

2 lbs. cubed venison
dash pepper
½ tsp. salt
1 beaten egg
2 tbsp. flour
1 clove garlic, crushed
½ cup salad oil
1 cup chicken bouillon

3 large green peppers
1 can (8-oz.) pineapple chunks
½ cup sugar
2½ tbsp. cornstarch
½ cup vinegar
2 tsp. soy sauce
cooked rice

Chop and boil peppers approximately 3 minutes, drain, and set aside. Batter venison chunks in mixture of flour, egg, salt, and pepper. Brown the meat in oil and garlic in a frypan. Remove venison and retain 1 tablespoon of cooking oil in pan.

Return venison to pan and add ⅓ cup of chicken bouillon; simmer for 10 minutes. Add pineapple and peppers. Combine sugar, cornstarch, vinegar, and soy sauce with remaining bouillon and add to frypan. Cook, stirring constantly, until mixture is thick and hot. Serve over rice. Yields six servings.

# Venison Teriyaki

2 lbs. venison steaks, ¼ in. thick
2 tbsp. lemon juice
1 can beef consommé (undiluted)
2 tbsp. brown sugar
1 tsp. savory salt

¼ cup green onions, including
    tops, chopped
1 clove garlic
⅓ cup soy sauce

Cut steak into ¼-inch strips diagonally across the grain. Combine other ingredients, pour over meat strips, and marinate in refrigerator overnight. After draining, broil about 4 inches from heat until tender. Serves four.

# Venison Spaghetti

2 lbs. ground venison
½ lb. smoked bacon
2 large onions, finely chopped
4 beef bouillon cubes
3 cans tomato sauce

oregano or Italian seasoning
salt and garlic powder
2 bay leaves
Parmesan cheese

Fry bacon and drain; cook onions and venison until done. Add tomato sauce, bouillon cubes, oregano, salt, garlic powder, and bay leaves. (Save Parmesan cheese to sprinkle over finished product.) Simmer low and long to blend the flavors.

Boil spaghetti noodles in salted water until tender; then drain and wash. Serve sauce generously over these noodles and sprinkle Parmesan cheese over all.

# Roasted Deer Heart

Marinate overnight. Wrap hearts with slices of salt pork. Roast over coals and hickory chips for 1 hour.

# Venison Ragout

2 lbs. marinated venison cubes
1 can beef consommé

1 cup raisins or chopped pecans
½ cup sherry

Sear venison in hot fat and add consommé. Simmer 30 minutes, at which time you may add 1 cup of raisins or chopped pecans. Simmer an additional 30 minutes and add sherry. Let steep for 5 minutes and serve on mashed potato mounds. Serves four.

# Large Game Marinade

1 lb. onions, chopped
½ head celery with tops, chopped
1 lb. carrots, chopped
1 qt. red wine
1 qt. vinegar

1 tbsp. tarragon
1 tsp. whole cloves
4 bay leaves
1 tsp. salt
1 tsp. whole peppercorns

Sauté vegetables in 1 cup bacon fat. Add remaining ingredients, boil, and simmer covered for ½ hour. Cool and store in refrigerator. Never add meat to hot or even warm marinade.

# Large Game Stew

assorted game cut in 1½-in.
  cubes
½ cup uncooked wild rice
½ cup celery, chopped
6 onions

½ lemon
2 bay leaves
4 tbsp. tomato sauce
2 tbsp. bacon fat or butter

Dredge game cubes in flour and brown in hot fat. Place in adequate covered pot. Sauté rice and celery in pan drippings until rice is browned. Add 2 cups water and boil about 15 minutes. Add to meat along with remaining ingredients. Cover with water and cook, covered, over low heat about 3 hours or until meat is tender. Thicken with mixture of cornstarch and hot water. Serve over egg noodles or fluffy rice.

## Swiss Venison Steak

1½ lbs. venison round steak,  
   1½ in. thick  
½ cup flour (approximately)  
salt and pepper to taste  
¼ cup fat

3 large onions  
1 cup tomatoes  
1 stalk celery, medium  
2 tbsp. Worcestershire sauce

Salt and pepper venison, lightly flour, and brown in fat on both sides. Add remaining ingredients, cover, and cook about 1 hour, until tender, either over low heat on top of stove or in 350-degree oven. Serves four.

## Chuka Chaha Roast Venison

5 lb. venison roast

BASTING SAUCE  
butter  
Worcestershire sauce

lime juice (or lemon)  
salt and pepper

Barbecue roast over a low hickory fire for 2½ hours, basting often. As meat browns, cut off the brown slices and mop on your favorite barbecue sauce. Continue cutting the meat until all is cut. This method gives you brown outside meat all the way through. Serves ten.

# Bear Round

4 bear round steaks
3 tbsp. butter
3 sliced onions
1 clove pressed garlic
1 tbsp. Worcestershire sauce

2 tbsp. ketchup
1 tsp. prepared mustard
salt and pepper to taste
1 cup water

Sauté onions in butter until tender. Add all ingredients except steaks. Simmer 15 minutes. Broil steaks until done to taste. Serve with sauce poured over and topped with sautéed bell peppers and/or mushrooms.

# Bear Stew

1½ lbs. bear meat, cut in 1½-in. cubes
flour
1 cup dry red wine
4 beef bouillon cubes
2 small bay leaves

4 cups water
1 clove garlic, crushed
salt and pepper to taste
4 carrots, cut in 1-in. pieces
4 onions, cut into halves
8 very small potatoes, whole

Marinate meat 2 hours in Marinade 3 (see recipe). Dredge in flour and sear in skillet with bacon fat. Add next six ingredients and cook slowly in covered pot about three hours. Add more water if necessary. About 1 hour before meat is done, add vegetables and cook until done.

# Bear Steak in Casserole

bear steak
4 cloves pressed garlic
dash cayenne pepper

½ tsp. chili powder
4 onions, sliced
2 cups tomato juice (or V-8)

Marinate steak for 3 hours, wipe dry, and sear on both sides in a medium-sized pot with bacon fat. After searing, add the garlic, cayenne, and chili powder to the pot. Cover and simmer for about 2½ hours.

Add the onions and tomato sauce; continue to cook until the onions are tender. Thicken sauce, if desired, with a mixture of cornstarch and water.

## Bear a la Frank

MARINADE
*1 part red wine*
*1 part oil*
*2 tbsp. soy sauce*

*½ lb. bacon*
*2 large onions, sliced*
*2 green peppers, sliced round*
*1 cup prepared mustard*
*½ lb. brown sugar*
*onion powder*

*2 tbsp. Worcestershire sauce*
*garlic powder*
*salt and pepper*
*4 cups water*
*6 beef bouillon cubes*

Marinate roast 2 to 3 hours. Rub salt, pepper, onion powder, and garlic powder on meat. Place roast on rack in Dutch oven and cover with bacon slices.

Combine sugar, mustard, and Worcestershire sauce and pour over meat. Add water and bouillon cubes to bottom of pan. Cover and cook at 300° for approximately 4 hours, basting often and adding more water if necessary. About 1 to 1½ hours before done, add sliced onions and peppers.

# Bear Pot Roast

1 bear rump roast
flour
salt
pepper
3 tbsp. bacon fat
1 qt. water

6 chicken bouillon cubes
6 very small potatoes, whole
4 carrots, cut in 1-in. pieces
4 medium onions, halved
8 small fresh mushrooms

Marinate roast 4 hours in Marinade 1 (see recipe). Remove and dry. Rub in salt and pepper and dust with flour. Add 2 tablespoons salt to Dutch oven and sear roast on all sides. Add fat, bouillon cubes, and water. Cover and cook at 350° until tender (about 30 minutes per pound). About 1 hour before meat is done, add remaining ingredients.

# Unsuccessful Hunter's Stew

1 clove garlic, pressed
1 cup quartered onion
1 cup sliced carrots
6 slices bacon, diced
3 cups beef bouillon or stock

¼ cup red wine vinegar
salt and pepper to taste
2½ lbs. stew beef
1 green pepper, sliced
¾ cup uncooked rice

After cooking bacon in skillet, remove pieces and set aside. Leave only a coating of fat in the skillet in which to sauté onions until soft. Add carrots and garlic and sauté. Add reserved bacon pieces, vinegar, 2 cups beef stock or bouillon, salt, and pepper. Bring to a boil; cover and simmer for 2 hours. Turn heat up; add pepper, rice, and remaining beef stock or bouillon; bring to a boil. Cover and simmer 20 to 25 minutes until rice is cooked. More stock may be added if necessary. Yields four to six servings.

# Sausage Stuffing Balls

1 lb. fresh pork sausage
1 pkg. (7 to 8 oz.) seasoned
  stuffing mix
¾ cup hot water

½ cup finely chopped onion
½ cup finely chopped celery
1 egg, beaten
½ tsp. baking powder

Combine stuffing mix with hot water. Break sausage into small pieces and add to moistened stuffing mix. Stir in onion, celery, egg, and baking powder until evenly distributed. Shape into balls, using ¼ cup of the mixture for each ball, and place in a baking pan. Cover with foil, securing tightly around pan.

Bake in a slow oven (325°) for 15 minutes. Remove foil; increase oven temperature to 350° and continue baking for 25 minutes or until sausage is done. Makes 18 to 22 balls.

# Pork and Sauerkraut

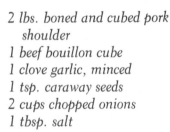

2 lbs. boned and cubed pork
  shoulder
1 beef bouillon cube
1 clove garlic, minced
1 tsp. caraway seeds
2 cups chopped onions
1 tbsp. salt

1 tsp. dried dill weed
1 tbsp. paprika
2 cups sour cream
1 can (1 lb., 11 oz.) drained
  sauerkraut
cooked potatoes

In a saucepan, combine the first seven ingredients and bring to a boil. Cover and simmer for 1 hour. Add paprika and sauerkraut and simmer again for 1 hour or until meat is tender.

Turn heat off; add sour cream gradually. Heat mixture thoroughly and serve with cooked potatoes. Yields six servings.

# Cheese Corned Beef Hash

1 lb. corned beef hash
1 onion, chopped
½ lb. diced sharp cheddar cheese

2 tbsp. fat
1 green pepper, chopped

Sauté onion and pepper in fat, add hash, and cook until browned. Add cheese and cook until cheese is partially melted. Makes four servings.

# Pork and Cabbage

1½ lbs. pork, cubed
2 tbsp. olive oil
2 tbsp. butter or margarine
1 medium cabbage, shredded
1 clove garlic, crushed
¾ cup minced onion

2 cups peeled and chopped
   tomatoes
⅓ cup minced green pepper
½ tsp. thyme
salt and pepper to taste

In a frying pan, brown pork in butter and oil. Remove pork and cook onion, garlic, and peppers until soft. Add tomatoes, salt, pepper, and thyme. Add pork cubes, cover, and simmer 30 minutes. Add cabbage and cook uncovered for 5 to 10 minutes, until cabbage is slightly cooked but still crisp. Serves four.

# Savory Lamb Chops

4 shoulder lamb chops, 1 in. thick
¼ cup chopped onion
2 tbsp. olive oil
salt and pepper to taste
⅓ cup dry sherry

1 cup peeled and chopped
   tomatoes
½ cup sliced carrots
1 cup sliced mushrooms
2 tbsp. butter

Salt and pepper chops and brown with chopped onion in oil. Add sherry, carrots, and tomatoes and simmer, covered, for 1 hour or until tender. Sauté mushrooms in butter and add to chops, cooking mixture an additional 5 minutes. Four servings.

## Barbecue Short Ribs

4 large beef short ribs
2 tbsp. cooking oil
½ cup diced celery
1 clove garlic, minced
½ cup diced onions
dash pepper
1 tsp. salt

½ tsp. allspice
1 tbsp. vinegar
1 tbsp. prepared mustard
1 tbsp. sugar
1 can (8 oz.) tomato sauce
2 tbsp. cornstarch

Brown ribs in oil. Add next three ingredients; mix tomato sauce with cornstarch and add to ribs. Stir in remaining ingredients and ½ cup water, cover, and cook slowly (1½ to 2 hours), turning occasionally. Serves four.

## Pork Loin Roast

pork loin, 4 to 6 lbs.

Place roast, fat side up, on rack in open roasting pan. Insert roast meat thermometer so that the bulb is centered in the thickest part. Make certain the bulb does not rest in fat or on a bone. Do not add water; do not cover.

Roast in a slow oven (325°) until the thermometer registers 170°. Allow 30 to 45 minutes per pound for roasting a center loin; 30 to 45 minutes per pound for a half loin; and 40 to 45 minutes per pound for an end roast (total time 2 to 3 hours).

# Vermouth Pork Chops

6 pork chops
¼ tsp. pepper
1 tsp. salt
½ tsp. thyme
¼ cup flour

2 tbsp. salad oil
2 tbsp. butter or margarine
½ cup dry vermouth or dry white
   wine

Batter pork chops in mixture of flour, pepper, salt, and thyme. Brown in melted oil and butter. Drain off fat from skillet and add vermouth or wine. Simmer about 30 minutes or until chops are tender. Add more wine if necessary during cooking. Makes enough for six.

# Gourmet Pork Chops

4 loin pork chops, 1 in. thick
¼ cup chopped parsley
3 tbsp. shortening
½ cup dry bread crumbs

½ cup fresh chopped mushrooms
4 slices Swiss cheese, diced
1 egg, beaten
½ cup Chablis

Slit each pork chop from bone almost to fat and stuff with a mixture of cheese, mushrooms, and parsley. Dip each chop in egg, then into bread crumbs.

    Melt shortening in skillet and brown chops. Add Chablis and simmer for 45 minutes or until meat is tender. Remove chops, season sauce with salt and pepper, and pour over meat.

# Barbecued Gator

alligator fillets
seasoned salt
oil

lemon juice
barbecue sauce

Liberally sprinkle the alligator meat with seasoned salt. Marinate the fillets in an adequate amount of oil and lemon juice for 3 hours. Arrange the fillets on a well-oiled grill above a low charcoal fire that is laced with soaked hickory chips. Grill in this slow fashion until the fillets are golden brown, occasionally basting with the lemon and oil marinade. When they are done, brush with the barbecue sauce and cook another 15 minutes.

# Smoked Gator

alligator fillets
salt and pepper

paprika
prepared Italian dressing

Alligator is excellent when smoked in the traditional manner. Season the gator fillets with salt, pepper, and paprika; marinate in the prepared Italian dressing for 2 hours. Cover fire with soaked hickory chips and smoke over low heat for about 3 hours or until completely done.

# Fried Gator Fillets

8 ½-in. gator fillets
salt
1 cup buttermilk

1 cup self-rising flour
2 eggs, beaten well
1 tbsp. cooking oil

Soak fillets in buttermilk for 30 minutes, drain, and salt. Prepare a batter for the meat by mixing the remaining ingredients; add enough cold water to this mixture to attain the consistency of thin pancake batter. Dip each fillet into this batter and fry in medium hot peanut oil for 5 minutes.

Try this procedure with fish and very thin cube steaks.

# Alligator Chowder

alligator chunks
onions, sliced thin
Irish potatoes, sliced thin
smoked bacon

crumbled crackers
butter
cream
salt and pepper to taste

Lightly oil the bottom and sides of an adequate Dutch oven and place a layer of sliced bacon on the bottom. On top of this, layer first the alligator chunks, then the onions, potatoes, and top with crumbled crackers. Repeat the layers in the same order until the gator meat runs out. Add enough water to half-fill the Dutch oven. Cover and simmer slowly in oven until done. Add cream, re-cover, and cook in a moderate oven for 30 minutes.

# Creole Style Alligator

4 lbs. cubed gator meat
1½ tbsp. salt
4 dashes Tabasco
1½ bell peppers, diced
½ tsp. pepper
1 tbsp. lemon juice
1⅓ cup chopped onions
2 tbsp. packed brown sugar

⅔ cup white wine
2½ cups chopped celery
3 bay leaves
½ cup flour
8 whole cloves
½ cup butter
3 20-oz. cans tomatoes
2 tsp. Worcestershire sauce

Melt butter and add bell pepper, onions, and celery. Sauté about 10 minutes, or until tender. Remove from heat. Add flour and blend thoroughly. Add tomatoes gradually, stirring constantly. Add salt, pepper, sugar, bay leaves, and cloves. Bring to a boil, add gator meat, and boil again. Reduce heat and simmer, uncovered, about 45 minutes, stirring occasionally. Remove from heat and stir in Worcestershire sauce, Tabasco, lemon juice, and white wine. Serve over hot rice to fifteen diners.

NOTE: This recipe was obtained from A *Herpetological Cookbook* by Mr. Ernie Liner from Houma, Louisiana, with my many thanks.

# Fried Gator Tail

*boned gator tail*
*seasoned flour*
*butter*

Slice gator tail across the grain. Dredge in flour and fry in butter until brown and tender. Make a cream gravy if you like and immerse fried pieces. Serve with rice and hot biscuits.

# Rattlesnake Salad

*1 medium rattlesnake, cut up*
*2 bay leaves*
*2 cloves garlic*
*1 tbsp. salt*
*1 tsp. poultry seasoning*
*2 tbsp. sherry*

*½ stalk celery, finely diced*
*4 boiled eggs, diced*
*½ onion, finely diced*
*½ cup chopped sweet pickles*
*1 cup mayonnaise*

Combine the first five ingredients and boil until the snake is tender. Chop the meat finely and mix well with the remaining ingredients. Serve on sandwiches or over quartered tomatoes and lettuce.

# Fried Rattlesnake

*rattlesnake meat, cleaned and cut*
  *into 2-in. cubes*
*buttermilk*

*salt*
*pancake mix*

Soak the meat in salted buttermilk for 1 hour; drain. Dredge the meat cubes in the prepared pancake mix and fry 7 minutes in deep, hot fat. Drain well and serve with spinach or potato cakes.

# Creole Rattlesnake

1 medium rattler, cleaned and
  cut into bite-sized pieces
¾ cup flour
¼ cup butter
1 4-oz. can sliced mushrooms,
  including liquid
1 cup white wine
1 8-oz. can tomato sauce

½ tsp. ground basil
4 chicken bouillon cubes
1 onion, diced
2 green peppers, diced
¼ cup cornstarch
salt and pepper
paprika

Dredge rattlesnake meat in flour seasoned with salt, pepper, and paprika and brown in butter. Add mushroom liquid, wine, tomato sauce, basil, and bouillon cubes and simmer for 15 minutes. Stir in mushrooms, onion, and pepper. Cover and cook over low heat for 30 to 45 minutes or until meat is tender. Combine cornstarch with ½ cup water and stir into creole until thickened. Serve over rice.

# Fried Armadillo

1 armadillo (1 possum on
  the half shell)

seasoned flour
butter

Cut armadillo into serving-sized pieces. Dredge in seasoned flour and fry in butter until brown and tender. A cream gravy can be made and served with the armadillo.

# Baked Armadillo

1 armadillo
salt and pepper to taste
¼ to ½ cup butter

Rub armadillo with salt and pepper. Cover with butter, wrap in foil, and grill or bake in oven. Armadillo most closely resembles pork, so cooking time should be the same as for a fresh pork roast of the same size. When done, remove foil, add more butter, and brown.

## Barbecued Armadillo

1 armadillo
salt and pepper

¼ to ½ cup butter
barbecue sauce

Season and cook armadillo according to the instructions for baking. After removing foil, baste with your favorite barbecue sauce. Try Goolsby's Special Barbecue Sauce. (See recipe.)

## Fried Rabbit 1

rabbits, cut up for frying
salt and pepper to taste
¾ cup flour

Lightly dredge rabbit in flour containing salt and pepper. Fry in bacon grease over medium low heat.

## Fried Rabbit 2

2 rabbits
1 egg, beaten
dash nutmeg

2 lemons, juiced
salt and pepper to. taste
1 cup bread crumbs

Parboil rabbits for 10 minutes in water containing lemon juice. Drain and season with salt, pepper, and nutmeg. Dip in beaten egg and then in bread crumbs and fry in very hot deep fat. Drain by holding pieces over flame. Garnish with parsley and serve with your favorite vegetables.

# Best Bunny

1 rabbit, dressed and disjointed
2 onions, sliced
2 carrots, thinly sliced
2 potatoes, sliced

8 slices bacon
2 cups water
1 tsp. salt
pepper to taste

Soak rabbit in salt water for 2 hours. Wipe dry and dredge in flour. Fry bacon and remove from skillet; fry rabbit in fat. Arrange rabbit and vegetables in casserole and place bacon on top. Add water and seasonings. Bake covered about 2 hours at 350°.

# Jugged Hare

1 rabbit, cut up
¾ cup flour
2 medium onions, quartered
½ lb. diced bacon
1¾ cups beef broth
4 medium carrots, halved
2 sprigs parsley
½ tsp. rosemary leaves
1 qt. water
¼ cup melted red currant jelly
1 cup red Bordeaux wine

MARINADE
1½ cups red Bordeaux wine
1 medium onion, quartered
½ cup red wine vinegar
2 sprigs parsley
2 tbsp. salad oil
1 tsp. cracked bay leaves
¼ tsp. each, pepper, thyme,
    rosemary

Combine ingredients for marinade, pour over rabbit, cover, and refrigerate for 24 hours, turning occasionally. Drain and save marinade. Dredge rabbit with flour and brown in melted butter.

Place meat in Dutch oven or large pot with onions, bacon, broth, carrots, parsley, rosemary, water, and ½ cup of marinade. Cover and simmer 2 hours, or until tender.

Remove meat and add jelly and 1 cup wine to pot. Combine 1 tablespoon flour with remaining marinade and add to liquid while simmering. Return meat to pot and serve. Yields six servings.

# Hasenpfeffer

MARINADE

1 tbsp. mixed pickling spices
1 tsp. freshly ground pepper
1 cup dry red wine
3 bay leaves
1½ cups vinegar

2 tsp. salt
2 cups sliced onion
8 whole cloves
1½ cups water

2 medium rabbits, cut up
1½ cups flour
1 tbsp. sugar

⅓ cup butter
1½ cups sour cream

Combine ingredients for the marinade, pour over rabbit, cover, and refrigerate for 24 to 36 hours, turning three times. Remove rabbit, drain, and dust lightly with flour. Brown in melted butter. Strain marinade and add to rabbit. Bring rabbit to a boil; cover and simmer 45 minutes or until tender.

Remove rabbit, keeping it warm. Add sugar to liquid. Add flour to small amount of cooled liquid, using 1 to 1½ tablespoons for each cup of liquid. Recombine with remaining liquid and cook until smooth and thickened. Blend well, folding in sour cream, and pour over rabbit. Serves six to eight.

# Baked Rabbit

2 rabbits
2 to 3 tbsp. melted butter
salt and pepper to taste
1 medium onion, chopped
1 tsp. flour
1 bay leaf

1 cup mushrooms, chopped
1 sprig thyme
1 tsp. garlic, chopped
small amount parsley
1 cup boiling water

Coat rabbit with melted butter, salt, and pepper, and bake at 400° for 45 minutes.

Sauté onion in small amount of butter; as it starts to brown, add flour and continue cooking until well browned. Add to this the next five ingredients and simmer about 5 minutes. Add boiling water and simmer until smooth. Pour this mixture over rabbit and bake for 20 minutes, basting frequently.

# Squirrel Pie

1 squirrel, cut in 3 pieces
2 cups milk or stock
3 tbsp. flour
⅛ tsp. pepper
1 tsp. salt
½ tbsp. minced parsley
½ cup fresh cut mushrooms

PASTRY
2 cups flour
¼ tsp. salt
4 tsp. baking powder
⅔ cup milk
¼ cup shortening

Boil meat until tender; remove bones. Combine remaining ingredients and cook until thickened. Add meat and pour into a baking dish.

FOR CRUST: Sift dry ingredients together, cut in shortening, and add milk. Roll on floured surface until it is about the size of the baking dish. Cover baking dish and bake in a 500-degree oven about 8 to 10 minutes until done.

# Smothered Squirrel

4 squirrels
3 qts. boiling water
8 strips bacon

1 tbsp. vinegar
½ tbsp. cooking sherry
1½ tbsp. flour

Parboil whole squirrels until very tender. Remove and arrange in casserole. Remove enough of the stock to use as a base for gravy (1 to 1½
cups). Brown flour and add stock and vinegar. Cook until slightly
thick.

Sprinkle squirrels with flour and put bacon strips on top. Pour on
gravy and bake at 350° for 1 hour. Add sherry and continue baking for
15 minutes. Serve with rice cooked in remaining stock.

# Squirrel and Dumplings

DUMPLINGS
2 cups all-purpose flour, sifted
1 tsp. salt
1 cup milk

3 tsp. baking powder
3 tbsp. shortening

2 squirrels, cut up
salt and pepper to taste

Simmer seasoned meat in a covered pot of hot water until very tender.
Meanwhile, for the dumplings, sift the dry ingredients together and
then cut in the shortening until the mixture resembles coarse meal.
Add milk and mix with a fork until blended.

When the meat has become tender, bring the water to a boil. Drop
the dumplings by a tablespoon onto pieces of meat (dumplings dropped
in the water will be soggy) and cook uncovered for 10 minutes, with the
liquid bubbling. Cover and simmer for 10 minutes longer.

# Fricasseed Squirrel

1 squirrel, cut up
3 slices bacon, chopped
½ tsp. salt
⅛ tsp. pepper

⅓ cup broth
1 tbsp. sliced onion
1½ tsp. lemon juice
½ cup flour

Rub squirrel pieces with salt and pepper, roll in flour, and fry with bacon until done. Add remaining ingredients and simmer slowly for 2½ to 3 hours. Serves 4.

NOTE: Instead of lemon juice and bacon, you may use ⅛ teaspoon cayenne, 2 cups broth, 1 tablespoon paprika and 1 slice of sour apple.

# Roast Stuffed Coon

1 cup wine
baking soda
3 stalks celery, chopped
2 tbsp. chopped parsley

3 onions, chopped
2 carrots, chopped
3 chicken bouillon cubes
salt and pepper

Combine the wine, 2 tablespoons of salt, and 2 quarts of water into a large pot. Parboil the coon in this mixture for 1 hour. Sprinkle coon with baking soda, rub in, and rinse in cold water several times. Place in Dutch oven and barely cover with water. Add remaining ingredients, cover, and simmer for 30 minutes. Remove coon and rub with salt and pepper when cool. Remove fat from broth, strain, and save 1 cup for dressing.

Stuff coon with dressing and sew together. Place coon on rack in pan on back, add a little water, cover, and cook about 2 hours (or until tender) at 350° to 375°. Baste frequently, adding more water if necessary and occasionally drawing off fat. Before serving, remove from pan and brown under broiler.

# Roast Possum

1 possum, cleaned
¾ tsp. pepper
1½ tbsp. salt
¼ tsp. Worcestershire
1 tbsp. fat
1 hard cooked egg

1 cup bread crumbs
8 slices bacon
1 large onion, chopped
1 possum liver, chopped
   (optional)

Rub possum with 1 tablespoon of the salt and all of the pepper. Sauté onion in fat, add liver (if desired), and cook until tender. Add ¼ cup water, bread crumbs, egg, remaining salt, and Worcestershire sauce. Mix well and stuff possum; sew and truss as a fowl.

Put the possum in a roasting pan, place bacon across it, and pour 1 quart of water into pan. Roast uncovered in a 350-degree oven until tender (about 2½ hours). Baste with natural juices every 15 minutes. Serves six to eight.

# Roast Squirrel

1 squirrel
1½ tbsp. tarragon vinegar or
   lemon juice
1½ tsp. salt
1 tsp. onion juice
1 cup mushroom buttons

1 cup bread crumbs
1 tsp. melted fat
2 cups brown meat broth
¼ tsp. pepper
¼ cup cream

Clean squirrel and rub with 1 teaspoon of the salt, ⅛ teaspoon pepper, and then with lemon juice or vinegar. Combine cream, bread crumbs, onion juice, mushrooms, and the remainder of salt and pepper. Stuff squirrel with this mixture, sew, and truss. Roast in a moderate oven until almost done. Place bacon strips liberally on top and complete roasting.

# Squirrel Stew 1

2 qts. boiling water
1 squirrel, cut up
1½ tsp. salt
½ tsp. pepper
1 small onion, chopped
1 cup lima beans

2 potatoes, chopped
1 cup corn
1½ tsp. sugar
2 cups tomatoes
¼ cup butter

Combine first eight ingredients and simmer, covered, for 2 hours. Add sugar and tomatoes and simmer 1 hour. Pour in butter and simmer 15 minutes. Bring to a boil, remove from heat, and serve.

# Squirrel Stew 2

8 squirrels, pressure cooked
4 medium chopped onions
10 large potatoes, chopped

Cook meat until tender; remove bones. Cook onions and potatoes for 30 minutes. Mix all ingredients and cook until well done. Season with salt and pepper to taste.

# Williamsburg Game Pie

1 duck (4½ to 5½ lbs.)
2 lbs. rabbit
2½ lbs. venison
½ cup vegetable oil
2 cups port wine
1½ qts. brown sauce (See recipe.)
1 tbsp. Worcestershire sauce
1 clove garlic, minced
½ tsp. crushed black pepper

1 cup currant jelly
1½ lbs. quartered mushrooms
½ cup butter
1 lb. bacon, cut in ¼-in. cubes
1 can (15½ oz.) pearl onions
pastry crust mix (See recipe.)
2 eggs
¼ cup milk

Preheat oven to 400° F. Salt cavity of duck and place on a rack in a shallow roasting pan, breast side up. Bake 30 minutes, reduce heat to 325° and bake until done. Boil rabbit 1 hour, or until tender.

Cut venison in large cubes and sauté in the oil until well browned. Remove venison and drain oil from pan. Add wine to the pan and boil for 2 to 3 minutes, scraping down any brown particles. Return venison to pan and add brown sauce. Simmer for 45 to 60 minutes or until tender.

Cut the duck and rabbit in medium-sized pieces and place in the pan with venison. Season with Worcestershire sauce, garlic, pepper, and currant jelly.

Sauté the mushrooms in butter until lightly browned. Fry bacon until crisp; drain. Heat onions and drain. Divide mixture into individual casserole dishes and garnish the top of each with mushrooms, bacon, and onions. Cover with pastry crust, trim edges, and prick tops to allow steam to escape. Beat eggs lightly with milk and brush over the tops of the pies. Bake in a 350-degree oven for 20 to 25 minutes or until crust is golden brown.

## Beef Stock

10 lbs. beef bones
3 medium onions, chopped
2 ribs of celery, chopped
¼ cup oil
2 carrots, chopped
2 cloves garlic

1½ cups whole canned tomatoes
½ cup tomato puree
½ tsp. leaf thyme
½ tsp. black pepper
1 bay leaf

Preheat oven to 400° F. Brown bones in oven for about 45 minutes. Remove, drain fat, and place bones in a large soup pot. Heat oil in an iron skillet. Add onion, celery, carrots, and garlic; brown.

Remove the oil and add the browned vegetables, tomatoes, tomato puree, and seasonings to the pot of bones. Cover with cold water and bring to a boil. Reduce heat and simmer, uncovered, 6 to 8 hours. Strain stock through a double thickness of cheesecloth.

Stock can be frozen in cubes for future use. Makes 2 to 3 quarts.

## Brown Sauce

¼ cup butter
1 cup all-purpose flour
½ cup tomato puree
2 qts. hot beef stock

1 tbsp. hot beef bouillon
1 tbsp. bottled brown gravy sauce
salt to taste
caramel color (optional)

Melt butter and add flour, stirring constantly, until mixture is chestnut brown. Add tomato puree and stir well. Gradually add hot stock and bouillon, using a wire whisk to insure smoothness.

Boil, and then reduce heat to the lowest degree possible. Simmer for 2 hours or until the sauce has been reduced to about 1½ quarts. Add bottled brown gravy sauce, salt, and caramel color, if desired. Remove from heat and strain through a fine sieve. Cool to room temperature and refrigerate.

## Pastry Mix

3 cups all-purpose flour
1 tsp. salt
2 tsp. sugar

1 cup shortening
ice water

Mix dry ingredients together. Blend in shortening until it is the consistency of small pebbles. Store in a covered container in refrigerator.

Moisten the mix with enough ice water to hold the dough together when pushed lightly with fork. Roll out on a lightly floured board or pastry cloth. For prebaked crust, line pan with crust, prick well with fork, and bake at 425° F. for 12 to 15 minutes. Makes 4½ cups.

|  | SINGLE CRUST | DOUBLE CRUST |
|---|---|---|
| 8″ pie | 1-1¼ cups mix | 2-2¼ cups mix |
| 9″ pie | 1½ cups mix | 2½ cups mix |
| 10″ pie | 1¾ cups mix | 2¾ cups mix |
| 12 tart shells | 2¾ cups mix | |

# Wildfowl and Poultry

BIRDS ARE VERY EASY to prepare and are always a hit. I prefer quail. I get a lot of pleasure from hunting them and even more pleasure in preparing them. My freezer is well stocked after the season is over.

Chicken is economical, if you're concerned about that and can be enjoyed by all, from those with a taste for the simple to those who boast of a very delicate taste bud.

## Down-Home Quail

4 quail
salt and pepper to taste
1 stick butter

8 small potatoes
4 small onions
4 chicken bouillon cubes

Rub quail with salt and pepper. Place ¼ stick butter and 1 bouillon cube in the body cavity of each quail. Place 4 potatoes, 2 onions, and two of the four quail in heavy aluminum foil, tightly closed but loosely wrapped; wrap the other two quail in the same manner with the remaining ingredients. Place in the live coals and ashes of an open fire. Add new coals occasionally and remove in about 2½ hours. Delicious!

## Baked Quail

4 quail
1 cup sliced mushrooms
salt and pepper to taste

½ cup melted butter
4 slices bacon

Rub quail with salt and pepper. Wrap a slice of bacon around each quail and place in a baking dish. Cover with foil and bake at 450° F. until tender (about 30 minutes). Remove foil, baste with butter, add mushrooms, and roast until brown. Baste once or twice while roasting.

# Fried Quail 1

4 quail
1 cup buttermilk
2 chicken bouillon cubes

1½ cups flour
1 tsp. poultry seasoning

Dissolve bouillon cubes in buttermilk and soak quail for 10 minutes. Dredge in mixture of flour and poultry seasoning and fry until brown and tender. Make a cream gravy. Don't forget the biscuits!

# Fried Quail 2

4 quail
salt and pepper to taste
1½ cups flour

Roll quail, either whole or in halves, in flour mixed with salt and pepper and fry in deep, hot fat until brown and tender. The quail may be seasoned with salt and pepper and fried with the flour coating either in butter alone or also with mushrooms.

# Quail Chasseur

4 quail
pinch of thyme
¼ cup butter
10½ oz. condensed consommé

2 tbsp. flour
½ bay leaf
½ cup white wine
salt and pepper to taste

Rub quail with salt and pepper, inside and out. Brown in butter and sprinkle over with flour. Add wine, thyme, bay leaf, and consommé; cover, and simmer until tender (about 45 minutes). Serve quail with pan juices spooned over. Yields four servings.

# Quail and Wild Rice

5 quail
1¼ sticks butter
1 clove garlic, minced
1 large onion, chopped
¾ lb. chicken livers

1 small green pepper, chopped
1 cup chicken broth
¾ cup port wine
1¼ cups cooked wild rice

Sew body cavity of quail together. Sauté in ½ stick butter until brown. Place in a baking dish and bake for 30 minutes at 325° F. Sauté the next four ingredients in ¾ stick butter until clear. Add remaining ingredients, place in baking dish and bake, covered, at 325° F. for 20 minutes or until the liquid is absorbed. Serve quail over this rice mixture. Serves four to five.

# Smothered Quail

6 quail
½ cup sherry
2 cups chicken broth

6 tbsp. butter
3 tbsp. flour
salt and pepper to taste

Brown quail in melted butter in a large skillet. Remove quail and place in a baking dish. Add flour to the butter remaining in the skillet, stirring well. Combine chicken broth, sherry, salt, and pepper; mix well and pour over quail. Bake, covered, for 1 hour in a 350-degree oven. Serve with cooked rice. Makes enough for six.

# Roasted Quail with Mushrooms

4 quail
4 slices bacon
½ cup hot water

¼ cup lemon juice
⅓ cup chopped mushrooms

Bacon-wrap each quail, securing with toothpicks or skewers. Place in a shallow, buttered pan and bake for ½ hour at 350° F. Baste often with mixture of water and lemon juice. When tender, remove and add mushrooms. Heat and serve with rice and gravy or on toast. Serves four.

# Braised Quail with Bacon

6 quail
2 tbsp. butter
½ cup hot water

18 strips bacon
4 tbsp. flour

Prepare quail for cooking and let stand overnight in refrigerator. Before cooking, place quail in salted water for 15 minutes (use one tablespoon of salt to each quart water). Drain and dry with a cloth. Place one strip of bacon in the body cavity, one across the back, and one across the legs.

Place quail in baking dish and bake at 450° F. for 5 minutes. Reduce heat to 350° F. and continue cooking for about 45 minutes. Baste frequently with mixture of butter and water. When tender, sprinkle quail with flour, return heat to 450° F., and brown for 10 minutes. Six servings.

# Sam's Smothered Doves

24 doves, picked and cleaned
2 tbsp. sherry
cornstarch

½ lb. smoked bacon
3 pts. boiling water
4 chicken bouillon cubes

Parboil doves until done. Arrange in an adequate casserole or pan, breast up. Place strips of bacon across the dove breasts after lightly sprinkling them with flour. Combine the water and bouillon cubes, thicken slightly with cornstarch, and pour liberally over doves.

Cook in a moderate oven (325° F.) for 30 minutes. Add sherry and raise temperature to 400° F.; bake uncovered until bacon is done. Serve over rice.

## Dove Breasts

8 dove breasts
1 orange, sliced
salt and pepper

2 lemons, sliced
Worcestershire sauce to taste

Brown breasts in butter. Add a little water and simmer, covered, for 20 to 30 minutes. Place breasts and drippings in a casserole. Add Worcestershire sauce, salt, and pepper to taste, and garnish with lemon and orange slices. Bake, covered, in a 325-degree oven for 1 hour. Baste occasionally.

## Doves and Wild Rice

12 doves
¼ cup butter or oil
1 onion, sliced
¾ cup red wine
2 cups tomato sauce

1 cup stewed fresh tomatoes
pinch of thyme or rosemary
salt and pepper to taste
1½ cups uncooked wild rice

Brown doves in butter. Add onion and sauté until tender. Add tomato sauce, tomatoes, wine, seasonings, and if necessary, enough water to cover birds. Cook over low heat for 1 hour. Prepare rice. Serve doves and sauce over rice. Serves three.

# Doves on Toast

12 doves
¾ cup dry white wine
1 cup water
1 tsp. salt
½ tsp. pepper

2 tbsp. butter
3 tbsp. flour
3 cups milk
4 slices toast

Brown doves in butter. Remove from skillet and place in a saucepan with wine, water, salt, and pepper. Cook until liquids are gone. Brown flour in the skillet birds were fried in, adding more butter if necessary. Gradually stir in milk to obtain desired thickness. Place doves on toast and cover with gravy.

# Dove with Brown Gravy

8 doves, cleaned and picked
salt and pepper

flour
milk (optional)

Add salt and pepper to flour and lightly batter doves. Brown in cooking oil. Remove from pan, leaving a small amount of cooking oil. Stir in flour and brown. Add water to make gravy; mixture may be thickened by adding milk.

# Quail Paprika

8 quail
½ tsp. pepper
1½ tsp. salt
4 tbsp. flour

¾ cup butter
4 tbsp. paprika
2 cans cream of mushroom soup
1 cup sour cream

Rub quail with salt and pepper, inside and out. Rub with 3 tablespoons of flour and brown in butter. Remove and place in a casserole.

Combine soup, paprika, and 1 can of water or milk and stir until blended. Pour over quail and bake, covered, at 350° F. for 30 to 45 minutes or until tender. Remove quail to platter.

Stir remaining flour into pan juices. Add sour cream and heat, but do not boil. Season with salt and pepper to taste and pour over the quail. Makes four servings.

## Quail in Dutch Oven

8 quail
½ cup butter
1 onion, minced
¾ cup chopped parsley
2 cloves garlic, crushed
1 green pepper, chopped
¾ cup dry white wine

4 chicken bouillon cubes
1 can tomato sauce
1 can mushrooms
pinch of rosemary
pinch of thyme
salt and pepper to taste

Brown quail in butter in a Dutch oven. Add the next four ingredients and cook until tender. Add wine, cover, and simmer for 15 minutes. Add remaining ingredients and simmer about 1½ hours. Serve over wild rice or noodles to four diners.

## Dove Pie

Brown the birds well in butter, cover with water, and add bay leaf, salt, and pepper. Simmer until tender and if more water is needed, add a little. Thicken gravy with flour. Place mixture in casserole and add 1 tablespoon sherry. Cover on top only with pie crust and bake until brown.

# Quail in Wine

8 quail
¾ cup butter
1 green pepper, chopped
2 onions, chopped
2 cloves garlic, minced
1 small bay leaf

2 cloves
1½ tsp. peppercorns
2 cups white wine
1¼ tsp. minced chives
salt and pepper to taste
2 cups cream

Melt butter and add pepper, onion, garlic, bay leaf, cloves, and peppercorns; cook for 15 minutes. Add quail and brown. Add remaining ingredients, except cream. Simmer about 45 minutes or until tender.

Remove quail and place in a deep dish. Strain sauce and add cream. Heat to almost boiling and pour over quail. Serves four.

# Dove Casserole

16 doves
2 stalks celery, finely chopped
1 medium onion, finely chopped
¼ cup finely chopped chives
salt and pepper to taste
½ cup evaporated milk
¾ cup water

1 can mushroom or cream of
   chicken soup
¾ cup sherry
1 cup small peas
3 chicken bouillon cubes
3 tbsp. butter

Arrange doves in a casserole and sprinkle with the next three ingredients. Add salt and pepper. Combine the next five items and pour over doves. Dot with butter and space bouillon cubes among birds. Bake about 2½ hours at 350° F.

Thicken gravy with a mixture of cornstarch and hot water. Serve with wild rice and 5-minute boiled broccoli, seasoned with salt and butter. Serves four.

# Duke Rogero's Wine Birds

12 doves
2 sticks margarine
½ cup chopped onion
4 tbsp. chopped celery tops

1 tsp. tarragon
2 cups dry white wine
salt to taste

Combine wine, margarine, onions, celery tops, and salt in a saucepan. Add birds and simmer, covered, for 20 minutes. Add tarragon, uncover, and simmer for 15 minutes. Makes three servings.

# Braised Dove

8 doves
⅓ cup butter
¼ cup flour

3 cups water
1 lemon
salt and pepper to taste

Melt butter; add flour, salt, and pepper. After flour is brown, add water and juice of the lemon. Bring mixture to a boil and pour over doves. Cook, covered, in a 325-degree oven until tender.

# Baked Dove in Sauce

8 doves
1 can condensed mushroom soup
parsley

celery salt
pepper
½ cup cooking sherry

Season doves with pepper and celery salt to taste. Brown in butter. Make a sauce of soup, sherry, and a little parsley. Pour sauce over doves in a casserole. Bake at 350° F. until tender, basting often.

# Baked Duck and Sauerkraut

3½ lbs. wild duck, dressed
1 tbsp. baking soda
2 tsp. salt
¼ tsp. black pepper
½ cup diced celery

1 cup chopped onions
¼ cup butter
4 cups sauerkraut
2 cups diced apples
1 tsp. caraway seed

Rub the birds well with the baking soda, then rinse birds inside and out and wipe dry. Sprinkle inside and out with salt and pepper.

Sauté the celery and onions in the butter until browned. Drain the sauerkraut, saving the juice. Combine the sauerkraut, apples, and caraway seed with the celery and onions. Mix well and stuff the ducks with the mixture.

Cover and bake for three hours at 350° F. Uncover during the last hour of the cooking to brown the duck. During the roasting, use the sauerkraut juice for basting. When the bird is done, remove it from the pan and make a gravy from the sauerkraut juice and drippings.


# Dennis' Duck

3 pieces celery
1 bell pepper, slivered
1 tsp. salt
½ jar cherries
1 orange
½ pt. Chianti wine

1 large onion, slivered
3 cloves garlic, pressed
1 tsp. pepper
1 small can pineapple
1 stick butter
2 large ducks

Place ducks in a roasting pan and bake for 10 minutes at 450° F. Remove and stuff with a cornbread stuffing. Combine all of the above ingredients, pour the mixture over the ducks, and bake, covered, for two hours at 300° F., removing every 15 minutes and basting with the juices and the mixture. Serve duck and gravy over wild rice.

# Canvasback in Wine

WINE MARINADE

3 cups port wine
4 whole cloves

1 large bay leaf
1 large onion, sliced

3 ducks
salt and pepper to taste
2 lemons
½ tsp. grated orange rind
juice of 3 oranges

2 sprigs thyme
1½ tsp. minced shallot
dash of cayenne
1½ cups chicken bouillon

Rub ducks inside and out with juice of 1 lemon and sprinkle with salt and pepper. Place in a large bowl, cover with marinade, and refrigerate for 24 hours.

Remove ducks; strain marinade. Combine 1 cup of marinade with the orange rind, orange juice, juice of remaining lemon, thyme, and shallots. Add cayenne and salt to taste.

Cook until reduced by half. Thicken slightly with a cornstarch and water mixture; add chicken bouillon. Place ducks on a rack in a roasting pan and brush with marinade. Cook about 1½ hours at 350° F., basting frequently. Serves six.

# Simple Roast Wild Duck

Prepare duck for cooking. Stuff and sew together. Place on a rack in a pan, breast side up. Cook, covered, for 1½ to 2 hours, at 350° F., depending on age and size, until tender. Uncover and cook at 450° F. until brown. Make basting sauce of 1 cup orange marmalade, 3 tablespoons prepared mustard, 1 cup sherry, and salt and pepper to taste. Baste with this and the pan drippings frequently during cooking time. Select a sauce from our sauce section to serve with this duck. The peach sauce complements this dish very well.

# Mallards with Mushroom Sauce

MUSHROOM SAUCE

1 can condensed cream of
  mushroom soup
1 can beef bouillon
2 cans water
½ tsp. salt

1 tsp. parsley flakes
½ cup sherry
½ tsp. Worcestershire sauce
¾ cup chopped mushrooms

4 mallards
½ cup flour
salt and pepper
¼ cup butter

1 onion, quartered
1 apple, quartered
1 orange, quartered

Rub ducks inside and out with salt and pepper, dredge in flour, and brown in butter. Remove birds and stuff with the onion, apple, and orange. Place in a roasting pan. Combine all sauce ingredients, cook until hot, and pour over ducks. Cover and bake for 1½ hours at 350° F., or until tender. Baste occasionally with sauce. Makes six servings.

# Onion Duck

2 ducks
½ lb. fresh mushrooms,
  sliced in half
2 onions, diced
¼ cup butter

½ cup sherry
salt and pepper to taste
paprika
1 can onion soup

In a deep skillet, sauté onion and mushrooms in melted butter until tender. Add ¼ cup sherry, cover, and simmer for 15 minutes. Split ducks in half, rub with salt and pepper, and add to skillet. Sprinkle with paprika. Add remaining sherry and onion soup. Cook, covered, for 45 minutes over medium heat.

# Wine Duck

2 ducks
salt and pepper
1 stalk celery

2 apples
½ cup butter or oil
1 cup sherry

Rub ducks with salt and pepper, both inside and out. Place 1 quartered apple and ½ stalk of celery in each duck. Sew cavity together.

Brown duck in butter or oil. Place on a rack in a roasting pan and add sherry. Bake, covered, for 1 hour at 425° F. Make a flour gravy with the pan drippings. This is great with apple and raisin salad and wild rice.

# Duck with Honey Sauce

2 ducks
1 tsp. pepper
4 tsp. salt
2 tsp. ground basil
2 tsp. ground ginger
½ cup butter
2 cups honey

¼ tsp. dry mustard
4 tsp. lemon juice
2 tsp. grated orange peel
6 tbsp. orange juice
2 oranges, unpeeled, cut into
    ½-in. slices

Combine pepper, salt, basil, and ginger and rub half inside the ducks. Heat together butter, honey, mustard, juices, and orange peel. Rub about 4 tablespoons of this mixture inside ducks. Stuff ducks with orange slices and pour 4 tablespoons of honey mixture into birds. Truss and rub remaining seasoning mixture over outside of ducks.

Place ducks on a rack in a roasting pan and cover with remaining honey mixture. Cover and bake for about 2 hours at 350° F. Uncover, baste with drippings, and bake until brown (about 20 minutes). Place on a platter. Thicken drippings with a water and cornstarch mixture. Stir, heat to boiling, and serve over ducks. Four servings.

# Roast Wild Duck

2 ducks
2 carrots, chopped fine
2 stalks celery, chopped fine
1 small can chopped ripe olives
¼ cup olive oil

salt and pepper
2 onions
½ cup chicken stock
½ cup port wine
1 tbsp. cornstarch

Combine the carrots, celery, and olives and sauté in olive oil for five minutes. Spread the mixture in a roasting pan and sprinkle with salt and pepper. Arrange the ducks on top and place an onion in each cavity. Brush liberally with olive oil and season with salt and pepper. Pour the chicken stock and wine around the ducks.

Roast in a hot (425° F.) oven for about 20 minutes. Place ducks on a serving platter and keep them warm. Strain the pan juices and thicken with cornstarch mixed with a little water. Serve the sauce separately. Four servings.

# Ducks in Fresh Mushroom Gravy

2 ducks, disjointed into serving
    size pieces
1 onion, sliced
½ cup butter or oil
1½ cups water

½ cup dry white wine
1 small bay leaf
salt and pepper
1 cup fresh mushrooms, sliced
2 tablespoons flour

Brown duck pieces in butter. Add onion and sauté until tender. Sprinkle meat with salt and pepper. Place in a Dutch oven along with water, wine, and bay leaf. Cover and cook over moderate heat for 1½ hours.

Sauté mushrooms in pan drippings. Stir in flour and brown slightly. Add enough milk to make a gravy of desired consistency. Pour over ducks and cook on low heat for about 45 minutes. Serve over rice.

# Shirley's Roast Goose

1 young goose                           poultry seasoning
salt and pepper to taste                butter

Sprinkle goose with salt, pepper, and poultry seasoning and rub thoroughly into meat. Stuff with your favorite stuffing. Place on a rack in a roasting pan, dot liberally with butter, and roast 30 minutes for each pound, basting frequently.

## Roast Goose 2

1 wild goose, cleaned
salt and pepper
¾ cup melted butter

APRICOT STUFFING                        GLAZE
2 cups dried apricots, steeped in       1 cup currant jelly
   hot water                            2 cups orange juice
2 tbsp. sugar                           6 tbsp. apricot brandy
2 cups bread crumbs

Parboil goose for 15 minutes. Remove, dry, and rub inside and out with salt and pepper. Combine stuffing ingredients with enough water to moisten and stuff goose. Place goose in roasting pan with butter and roast at 350° F. for 20 minutes per pound, basting frequently with butter.

   Combine glaze ingredients and heat. Pour over goose about 20 minutes before serving and continue to baste. Pour the remaining sauce into a gravy bowl. Serves six.

# Carrot-Stuffed Goose

1 Canadian honker,
  approximately 6 lbs.
2 cloves garlic
¼ cup melted bacon fat
6 strips thick smoked bacon

BASTING SAUCE:
pan drippings
1 cup dry red wine
1 tsp. basil

Rub goose inside and out with garlic, salt, and pepper. Stuff with Carrot Stuffing. (See recipe.) Cover goose with cheesecloth soaked in bacon fat. Place goose, breast side up, on a rack in a roasting pan and cover with bacon strips.

    Roast at 350° F. for 25 minutes per pound until tender, basting often. Add 1 cup water to roasting pan and cover during the last hour of cooking.

# Goose with Fruit and Nut Stuffing

1 wild goose, approximately 6 lbs.
salt and pepper
1 lemon, quartered
¼ cup melted bacon fat
6 strips thick, smoked bacon

BASTING SAUCE
½ cup orange marmalade
⅔ cup dry vermouth
½ tsp. nutmeg

Rub goose inside and out with garlic, salt, and pepper. Stuff with Carrot Stuffing. (See recipe.) Cover goose with cheesecloth soaked in skewers. Cover goose with cheesecloth soaked in bacon fat and cover with bacon strips. Place goose, breast side up, on a rack in a roasting pan and bake at 325° F. for about 25 minutes per pound. Baste often with sauce.

# Smoked, Glazed Chicken

½ chicken per person
salt and pepper
poultry seasoning

GLAZE

1 cup orange marmalade
2 tbsp. Worcestershire sauce
2 tbsp. vinegar
½ tsp. ginger
2 tbsp. bacon drippings

4 cloves garlic, crushed
4 chicken bouillon cubes (melted
  in water)
2 tbsp. ketchup

Rub meat with salt, pepper, and poultry seasoning. Grill over charcoal until done, and then place in a covered grill or smoker and smoke with hickory chips for 30 to 45 minutes.

Mix the glaze ingredients and simmer until blended. Brush the chicken with the glaze and place over the coals again; repeat this process several times.

Save this for your special guests.

# Southern Style Fried Chicken

Sprinkle chicken pieces with salt, pepper, and poultry seasoning. Dip into buttermilk and then into flour. Place in medium hot fat and cover. Cook each side done and place on paper towels to drain. Pour off all but 1½ tablespoons fat, saving also the browned flour from the chickens. Add one heaping tablespoon flour to hot fat and stir until browned well. Remove from heat 5 minutes and add 1 cup warm water stirring all the while. Now add enough milk to make thin gravy and place over medium heat until thickened. Salt and pepper to taste. Good as all outdoors.

# Chicken Maximilian

2 fryer chickens, quartered
¼ cup butter or margarine
1½ tsp. salt
1 tsp. paprika
2 tsp. minced onion
1½ cups orange juice

2 tbsp. grated orange rind
1 avocado
4 tsp. cornstarch
½ tsp. dried tarragon
½ tsp. ginger

After sprinkling chicken with salt and paprika, brown well in butter in a frying pan. Add tarragon, onion, ginger, orange juice, and orange rind. Cover and simmer for 30 minutes or until chicken is tender. Remove chicken to a heated platter.

Mix cornstarch with small amount of water and stir into sauce in pan, stirring constantly until mixture comes to a boil and thickens. Peel and wedge avocado and place around chicken. Pour some sauce over chicken. Pass around the remainder of sauce. Makes eight servings.

# Stewed Chicken with Dumplings

4-lb. stewing chicken, cut into
   serving pieces
1 carrot, diced
1 whole clove
1 small bay leaf

2 ribs celery, diced
1 medium onion, quartered
1½ tsp. salt
2 sprigs parsley
4 peppercorns

Place chicken in a deep pan, putting the less meaty pieces in first, and add boiling water to cover a little more than half. Add the remaining ingredients and bring to a boil. Cover and simmer, testing in about 2 hours for tenderness. Remove tender pieces and continue cooking until all is tender. Cooking time will average 3½ to 4 hours. Yields 6 servings. (See dumpling recipe in Bread Section.)

# Crisp Tote Chicken

2 fryers, cut up
2 cups buttermilk
1½ cups fine dry bread crumbs
⅓ cup grated Parmesan cheese
1 tsp. dry mustard

1 tsp. dried thyme
2 tbsp. chopped parsley
1 tsp. salt
¼ tsp. pepper
1 tbsp. corn oil

In a large mixing bowl, mix together the bread crumbs, Parmesan cheese, mustard, thyme, parsley, salt, and pepper. Dip chicken pieces first in the buttermilk and then in the bread crumb mixture. Line a 13-inch x 9-inch baking pan with foil and brush with oil. Place chicken skin side up in the baking pan. Bake at 375° F. for 1 hour. The chicken may now be refrigerated and later served as the main fare at your picnic.

# Country Captain

2 fryer chickens, cut into serving
    pieces
½ tsp. pepper
3 tsp. salt
½ cup flour
1½ cups butter or margarine
1 tbsp. curry powder

1 tsp. dried thyme
2 medium green peppers, chopped
2 cloves garlic, minced
2 medium onions, chopped
⅓ cup currants or raisins
2 cans (32 oz.) tomatoes

Dredge chicken in a mixture of flour, salt, and pepper and brown in melted butter in a frypan. Remove and add the next five ingredients, cooking until onions and pepper are tender. Return chicken, add tomatoes, and bring to a boil. Simmer, covered, for 15 minutes. Add currants or raisins, uncover, and simmer until chicken is tender (about 15 minutes). Eight servings.

# Chicken Elegante

1 jar sliced, dried beef
4 chicken breasts, split, skinned,
    and boned
1 cup sour cream
6 slices bacon, cut in half
1 can cream of mushroom soup

2 tbsp. chopped green onions
1 tsp. curry powder
4 tbsp. butter or margarine
4 cups cooked rice, unsalted
chopped parsley

In a shallow baking dish (13 inch x 9 inch x 2 inch) arrange a single layer of beef and then place the chicken breasts on top. Blend soup and sour cream and pour over; top with bacon, cover, and bake at 250° F. for 4 hours.

Uncover, stir soup, and bake for 1 hour more. Meanwhile, in a saucepan cook onion with curry in butter until tender and toss with rice. Serve chicken over rice and garnish with parsley. Makes four large servings.

# Fried Wild Turkey Breasts

1 pair or more wild turkey
    breasts, halved
flour

salt and pepper to taste
¼ cup bacon fat
milk

Slice turkey breasts about ¼ inch thick, across the grain. Pound breasts to tenderize, sprinkle with salt and pepper, and dredge in flour.

Fry in hot fat for about 1 minute on each side. Remove from pan and stir in 1 tablespoon of flour for each tablespoon of fat remaining. When smooth, stir in milk to make gravy of desired consistency. Add salt and pepper to taste and serve over fried breasts.

# Creamy Pheasant

1 pheasant, cut in
  serving-sized pieces
seasoned flour

shortening
1 cup cream (or 1 can cream of
  mushroom soup, ½ cup milk)

Coat pheasant pieces in flour and fry until brown. Pour cream in pan, cover, and cook over low heat until liquid is absorbed (about 1 hour). Remove from pan when tender and make a milk gravy with the drippings.

# Pheasant in Brandy

4 pheasants
½ cup butter
3 tbsp. minced onion
1 clove garlic, crushed
¾ cup brandy

salt and pepper to taste
2 cups chicken bouillon
1 pt. cream
2 tbsp. horseradish, prepared

Secure pheasants so they will not lose shape and brown in butter with garlic and onion. Place in a baking pan with the pan drippings. Pour brandy over and light; when the flame dies add salt, pepper, and bouillon.

Cover birds with the bacon and roast, uncovered, at 375° F. for 30 minutes, basting occasionally. Pour horseradish and cream over birds and continue baking for an additional 30 minutes, basting frequently. Place birds on platter and pour sauce over them. Serve with rice.

# Pheasant Pie

2 pheasants, skinned and
   cut in pieces
1½ qts. water
salt and pepper to taste

1 onion, diced
3 carrots, diced
1 bay leaf
1 can peas

Combine all ingredients except peas and cook until pheasant meat can be removed from bone. Remove meat and place in a buttered casserole. Add vegetables, including peas, and the stock, thickened with a mixture of water and cornstarch. Cover with your favorite biscuit recipe and bake until biscuit dough is brown (about 15 minutes at 475° F.).

# Glazed Stuffed Pheasant

Prepare pheasant as you would a roasting hen.

### STUFFING

1½ cups cooked rice
¼ cup butter
¼ cup finely chopped walnuts,
   pecans, or almonds

½ cup finely minced onion
salt and pepper to taste
½ tsp. poultry seasoning
2 tsp. sugar

Sauté onion and nuts in butter until onion is tender. Combine with remaining ingredients and stuff bird. Tie wings and legs.

### ORANGE GLAZE

1 cup orange juice
juice of 1 lemon
2 tsp. grated orange rind
¼ cup oil

¼ cup honey
2 tbsp. soy sauce
2 tbsp. Worcestershire sauce
½ cup vinegar

Combine above ingredients. Place pheasant on rack in pan breast side up and brush with glaze. Bake at 350° F. for 2 to 2½ hours, until bird is brown, basting frequently. About 30 minutes before bird is done, remove rack and lay slices from 2 oranges around pheasant. Continue cooking and basting until done. Serve with orange slices around bird and glaze poured over it.

## Sour Cream Pheasant

1 pheasant, cleaned and cut into
   serving-sized pieces
flour
⅓ cup butter

¼ cup minced onion
salt and pepper to taste
2 sprigs parsley, chopped
1 cup sour cream

Dredge pheasant pieces in flour and brown in butter along with the onion. Transfer pheasant, onions, and pan drippings to a baking dish. Add the remaining ingredients, cover, and bake at 350° F. for 1½ hours. Serves two.

## Pheasant with Apples

1 pheasant, cut into serving-sized
   pieces
salt and pepper to taste
⅓ cup butter

1 tbsp. cinnamon
1 cup apple cider
2 Golden Delicious apples, peeled
   and cut into chunks

In a Dutch oven, brown the pheasant in the butter. Add the remaining ingredients, cover, and simmer until tender (about 1 hour). Makes two servings.

# Teriyaki Pheasant

1 pheasant, split
⅓ cup butter

TERIYAKI MARINADE
¼ cup white wine
⅓ cup soy sauce
2 tbsp. sugar

¾ tbsp. grated ginger root
(or ⅓ tsp. powdered ginger)

Brown pheasant in butter and place in a shallow pan. Combine marinade ingredients, pour over pheasant, and marinate for 1 hour in refrigerator. Place each half of the pheasant on a piece of foil, cover with marinade, and seal. Cover each with a second piece of foil. Place in a shallow pan and bake at 325° F. for 1½ hours. Serves two.

# Cajun Pheasant

3 pheasants, cut into serving
  pieces
1 cup flour, seasoned with salt,
  pepper, and paprika
⅓ cup butter
½ tsp. ground basil
1 cup white wine

1 4-oz. can sliced mushrooms,
  including liquid
1 8-oz. can tomato sauce
3 green peppers, diced
2 onions, diced
4 chicken bouillon cubes

Dredge pheasant pieces in flour and brown in melted butter. Add basil, mushroom liquid, wine, tomato sauce, and more salt and pepper if desired. Cover and simmer for 15 minutes. Add remaining ingredients, cover, and cook over low heat until tender. Place pheasant on a platter and thicken sauce with a cornstarch and water mixture. Serve over rice to six to eight diners.

# Pheasant with Rice

2 pheasants
3 tbsp. bacon fat
5 tbsp. butter
1 cup wild rice
¼ tsp. ground ginger

½ tsp. salt
½ cup sliced mushrooms
3 cups chicken bouillon
1 stalk celery, chopped
1 onion, chopped

Disjoint the pheasants, setting aside the wings, necks, and backs. Brown the remainder of the meat in 3 tablespoons butter combined with the bacon fat. Sauté the mushrooms in the rest of the butter, cook the rice, and combine the two ingredients. Add ginger and salt.

Place rice on piece of heavy duty aluminum foil, top with pheasant meat, and seal. Bake 1½ hours at 350° F. Open and cook about 15 minutes.

Make the gravy by mixing the leftover pheasant pieces with the bouillon, celery, and onion in a saucepan. Bring to a boil and simmer about 30 minutes. Thicken with a cornstarch and water mixture; season to taste. Serve over pheasant and rice to four diners.

# Pheasant in Cream Sauce

1 pheasant
½ cup butter
½ cup milk

3 tbsp. flour
½ cup cracker crumbs

Place pheasant in a Dutch oven with enough water to cover; salt and pepper to taste. Cook at 375° F. until meat falls off bone (about 1 hour). Remove meat and place on an ovenproof platter.

To make gravy, brown flour in butter and stir until smooth. Add milk and stir until gravy thickens; add stock from pheasant. Season with additional salt and pepper if necessary. Pour sauce over pheasant, cover with cracker crumbs, dot with butter, and return to oven until butter melts. Makes two to three servings.

# Fried Grouse

grouse, cut into serving-sized
   pieces
evaporated milk

seasoned flour (with salt, pepper,
   and paprika)
cooking oil

Dip grouse in milk, coat with flour, and brown in oil. Cover and simmer about 30 minutes.

# Pan Grouse

grouse, cut into serving-sized
   pieces
seasoned flour
cooking oil
evaporated milk
1 cup mushroom soup
1 onion, finely chopped

1 cup sliced mushrooms
2 carrots, finely chopped
1 tsp. lemon juice
1 bay leaf
2 whole cloves
salt and pepper to taste
½ cup red wine

Prepare grouse in the same manner as fried grouse; when browned, add all ingredients except wine. Cover and cook until the vegetables are tender. Add wine and cook an additional 15 to 20 minutes.

# Grouse on a Spit

2 grouse giblets
2½ cups bread crumbs
½ cup butter
1 cup finely chopped celery
1 cup finely chopped onion
2 tbsp. grated orange peel

1 egg, beaten
salt, pepper, and poultry
   seasoning to taste
⅓ cup brandy
½ cup Italian dressing

Chop giblets and sauté them along with celery and onion in butter. Combine and add the remaining ingredients, except the Italian dressing and half of the brandy. Stuff the grouse, sew cavities closed, and place on a spit. Cook over medium heat for about 1 hour, basting frequently with the dressing. When done, remove and pour remaining brandy over the birds.

# Fried Goose Breasts

needed number of goose breasts, halved
flour

bacon fat
milk
salt and pepper to taste

Slice breasts to ¼-inch thickness across the grain. Tenderize, dredge in flour, and fry in bacon fat for about 1 minute on each side. Remove from skillet and stir in 1 tablespoon of flour for each tablespoon of bacon fat remaining. Brown flour and stir in milk until gravy is of desired consistency. Add salt and pepper and serve over goose breasts.

# Giblet Spaghetti

giblets from ducks or geese
olive oil
2 cloves garlic, crushed
1 bell pepper, finely chopped
2 onions, finely chopped

2 cups sliced mushrooms
1 tbsp. marjoram
½ tbsp. thyme
1 can mushroom sauce
2 cans tomato sauce

Chop giblets; combine with all ingredients, except tomato sauce and mushroom sauce, and sauté in oil until browned slightly. Add sauces and simmer about 1½ hours, adding water if necessary. Serve over cooked spaghetti noodles.

# Baked Pheasant in Milk

1 pheasant
⅓ cup butter
salt and pepper to taste

1 qt. milk
1 cup stuffing

Prepare pheasant as you would a whole turkey. Rub with salt and pepper, sauté in butter until light brown, stuff, and skewer closed. Place in roasting pan, add milk, and bake at 350° F. about 30 minutes for every pound. Baste frequently. Serves from two to three diners.

# Pheasant with Sauerkraut

2 pheasants, halved
½ cup butter
8 strips bacon
8 new potatoes, scrubbed
4 carrots, scraped and cut into
   thirds

2 onions, peeled and quartered
1 27-oz. can sauerkraut, drained
¼ cup dry white wine
½ tsp. cracked black pepper
1 tsp. caraway seeds

Parboil vegetables for about 10 minutes and drain. Brown pheasant halves in butter and remove. In the same pan fry 4 strips of bacon until almost crisp. Coat vegetables in some of the bacon fat and set aside.

Combine sauerkraut, wine, pepper, caraway seeds and remaining bacon fat. Crumble the cooked bacon into this mixture. Place half of this mixture in a casserole, top with the pheasant, and place the remaining sauerkraut around the pheasant. Arrange the vegetables around the meat and cover each pheasant half with a strip of bacon.

Bake, covered, at 350° F. for about 45 minutes. Uncover and bake another 30 minutes. Baste occasionally during the entire cooking time. Serves four.

# Fish and Seafood

# Batter-Dipped Fish

2 lbs. fish fillets or steaks
1 cup all-purpose flour, sifted
1 tsp. baking powder
⅔ cup milk

½ tsp. salt
2 eggs
2 tbsp. melted shortening

Sift dry ingredients together and add to mixture of milk and eggs. Add shortening. Dip fish, allowing each piece to drain slightly. Fry in hot shortening in skillet until brown (about 5 to 6 minutes). Drain and serve. Yields six servings.

# Sauce Elegante

¼ lb. cooked shrimp, finely chopped
⅓ cup dry white wine
1 can (10½ oz.) condensed cream of mushroom soup

1 tbsp. butter
dash black pepper
2 sprigs parsley, chopped
½ tsp. tarragon (optional)

Combine all ingredients in saucepan and heat. Pour over your favorite seafood dish. Makes 2¼ cups.

# Cocktail Sauce

2 tbsp. finely chopped celery
½ tsp. salt
1½ tbsp. horseradish
1 tsp. brown sugar

1 cup ketchup
1½ tbsp. lemon juice
1 tbsp. Worcestershire sauce

Combine all ingredients and chill.

# Marinated Fish

2 lbs. fish fillets
dry bread crumbs
⅓ cup tomato juice
1 tsp. Worcestershire sauce
¼ cup ketchup

¼ cup chopped onion
1 tbsp. vinegar
3 tbsp. lemon juice
dash pepper
½ tsp. celery salt

Combine all ingredients except fish and bread crumbs and cook 5 minutes. Cool and pour over fish. Marinate, covered, and refrigerate several hours. Remove fish, dip into bread crumbs, and fry until brown and tender. Six servings.

# Barbecued Fish Fillets

1 lb. fish fillets
5 tbsp. butter or margarine
salt and pepper to taste
½ cup diced onion
2 tsp. sugar

2 tsp. prepared mustard
½ cup ketchup
2 tsp. Worcestershire sauce
⅓ cup lemon juice

In 2 tablespoons of butter, sauté onions and then remove. Add remaining butter and brown the fish fillets. Spread onions over fish and season with salt and pepper. Combine ¼ cup water with the remaining ingredients, pour over fish, and simmer about 20 minutes. Serves four.

# Seafood Marinade

fish fillets or raw shrimp
¼ cup fresh lemon juice
½ cup salad oil
2 cloves garlic, crushed

1 tsp. ground ginger
1 tsp. grated lemon peel
¼ cup soy sauce
2 tsp. curry powder

Mix all ingredients. Place fish or shrimp in a bowl and cover with marinade. Let it stand at room temperature for at least 30 minutes.

Place shrimp or fish in a broiling pan 5 to 6 inches from the heat. Broil until done; occasionally baste with marinade.

# Chinese Shrimp Supper

2 tbsp. salad oil
½ lb. ground lean pork
½ lb. raw shrimp, shelled and
    halved
2 cups sliced mushrooms

1 tbsp. soy sauce
1 cup chicken stock
7 oz. partially thawed snow peas
⅓ cup minced scallions,
    including some green tops

Lightly brown pork in oil, add shrimp and scallions, and fry 2 minutes. Add mushrooms. Mix soy sauce and chicken stock, add to fry pan, and simmer 2 minutes. Add snow peas (edible pea pods) and cook 2 to 3 minutes until peas are thawed but still crisp. Serve with rice. Yields 4 servings.

# Catfish Chowder

1½ lbs. catfish fillets
½ cup chopped onion
1 cup diced potatoes
dash pepper
parsley flakes

3 tbsp. chopped bacon
    or salt pork
¾ tsp. salt
2 cups milk

Cut fillets into 1-inch pieces. Brown the bacon; add onion and sauté. Add water, potatoes, seasonings, and fish, cover, and simmer for 20 minutes. Add milk and heat. Garnish with parsley and serve six people.

# Fishmonger's Delight

2 lbs. fish
2 tsp. salt
1 lb. sliced bacon

2 tbsp. lemon juice
¼ tsp. pepper

Brush inside of fish with lemon juice and sprinkle with salt and pepper. Wrap each fish with bacon and place it in a well-greased, hinged wire grill 6 inches from coals for 15 minutes or until bacon is crisp. Turn and cook 10 minutes or until bacon is crisp. Serves six.

# Cedar Creek Shrimp Creole

2 lbs. shrimp
½ lb. smoked bacon, chopped
2 bay leaves
1 tsp. garlic powder
salt to taste
2 large cans tomatoes, mashed

½ stalk celery, chopped
2 green peppers
2 medium onions
1 tbsp. brown sugar
1 tbsp. chili powder

Cook bacon until brown; remove from skillet. Sauté vegetables and add cooked bacon. Meanwhile, boil and peel the shrimp and add all the other ingredients. Simmer for 1½ hours and serve over fluffy rice.

# Fried Frog Legs

frog legs
flour or bread crumbs
salt

Soak the frog legs in cold salted water for 15 minutes. Dry them with a paper towel and roll them in flour, bread crumbs, or your favorite frying batter. Fry in hot fat until golden brown and drain on paper towels.

# Shrimp Curry

2 lbs. shrimp, cooked and peeled  
1 large onion  
2 tbsp. butter or margarine  
1 pt. milk  
1 pt. half-and-half  
2 tbsp. chutney  

1 apple, chopped fine  
1 large tomato  
2 tbsp. flour  
2 tsp. curry powder  
salt to taste  

Melt butter in a heavy iron skillet or pot and add onions, apple, and tomato. Cook slowly until done and add flour and curry powder. Mix well. Add milk, half-and-half, chutney, and salt to taste. Cook slowly until thickened a little, stirring constantly. Add shrimp and heat slowly. Serve over hot rice with condiments (chopped green onions, chopped toasted nuts, chutney, or toasted coconut). Serves eight to ten.

# Shrimp and Rice Croquettes

1 cup rice  
2 eggs  
1 tbsp. butter or margarine  

2 lbs. shrimp, cooked and finely  
    chopped  

Cook rice. While hot, add butter, slightly beaten eggs, and then the finely chopped cooked shrimp. Season with salt and pepper and mold into croquettes. Dip into beaten egg and roll in finely crumbled saltines. Fry in deep fat.

# Scalloped Oysters

1 qt. oysters, including juice  
salt and pepper

bread crumbs  
butter

Drain and save the juice from the oysters; salt and pepper them to taste. Butter the bottom of a casserole dish and place in a layer of oysters and then a layer of bread crumbs and butter. Alternate these layers until the dish is full. Sprinkle bread crumbs on top and pour on a little of the oyster liquor. Bake at 250° F. until the bread crumbs are a light brown.

# Oyster Stew

1 pt. oysters, including liquid  
1 stick margarine  
1 small onion, finely chopped

1 pt. half-and-half  
1 pt. milk  
salt and pepper

Melt the margarine and sauté the chopped onion. Add oysters and liquor; let simmer until they curl. Add half-and-half and milk. Simmer (never boil) for 30 minutes. Salt and pepper to taste.

# Remoulade Shrimp

2 egg yolks, beaten  
½ pt. creole mustard  
¼ cup vinegar  
juice of 1 lemon  
salt and pepper to taste

1 pt. Wesson oil  
1 bunch green onions, minced  
½ stalk celery, minced  
4 lbs. shrimp, peeled and boiled

Blend together egg yolks, creole mustard, vinegar, lemon, salt, and pepper. Beat well. Slowly add Wesson oil, beating constantly. When sauce has thickened, add onions and celery. Soak shrimp in this sauce for about 4 hours. Serve on lettuce to six people.

# Snapping Turtle Stew
## (for large hungry groups)

3 gals. white cream style corn
2 gals. tomatoes
15 lbs. boiling potatoes
10 lbs. onions
salt and pepper to taste

30 lbs. turtle meat
2 hens
3 lemons
½ cup sherry

Boil turtle meat until reasonably tender; remove all bones. Do the same with the hens, but don't use the livers or gizzards. Peel both the potatoes and onions and boil until just tender enough to drain without coming apart.

With a good grinder (for relief of seldom-used muscles) grind the corn, tomatoes, potatoes, onions, and meat. Place all this in an adequate pot or cauldron. Squeeze lemons and drop rind halves into pot along with the juice and the sherry.

Cook slowly over medium heat while constantly stirring until done (approximately 1½ hours). Salt and pepper to taste about halfway through this cooking process, bearing in mind that the seasonings are somewhat accentuated as the flavors mingle and mix. Use a wooden paddle to stir; under no conditions allow the stew to stick.

This is an outstanding one dish meal. As an added embellishment corn on the cob may be added the last 30 minutes of cooking time. Serve with saltines or bread. Yields about 9 gallons.

This stew may be frozen (airtight) but don't scorch while warming.

# Stuffed Flounder

8 flounder fillets          2 lemons
1 lb. crabmeat              1 stick margarine
paprika

Soak flounder fillets in milk for 1 hour. Place 4 fillets on absorbent paper and arrange crabmeat on these. Place remaining 4 fillets on top. Press the edges down and bake 30 minutes at 350° F., basting often with lemon juice and butter. Sprinkle with paprika and broil until brown.

# Special Boiled Shrimp

In an adequate cauldron containing 2 gallons of water, place ¼ box salt, 2 bay leaves, 1 garlic clove, and 1 jar of prepared mustard. Bring to a boil and add 4 pounds of shrimp. Maintain the boil until the shrimp float and may be easily removed from the shell. Drain and place in the refrigerator on a damp pad of paper towels until cold and ready to eat with your favorite cocktail sauce.

I prefer to boil the medium to small shrimp and use the larger shrimp in various other fashions.

# Grilled Bream

Clean the bream in the normal manner, except when removing entrails cut the fish down the back, leaving the belly intact. Place cut side down over hot coals, with some applewood chips and hickory chips sprinkled liberally on the red-hot grill fire. When reasonably browned, you may salt fish and brush them with a lemon-butter mixture and turn over. Brush often and keep turning until pleasantly browned.

# Deviled Crab

1 lb. crabmeat
2 tbsp. chopped sweet pepper
1 tsp. dry mustard
1 tbsp. sherry
1 tsp. pepper
1 egg
½ cup plain bread crumbs
¼ cup chopped onion

¼ cup chopped celery
1 tsp. parsley
1 tbsp. salt
paprika
½ stick butter
2 heaping tbsp. flour
2 cups milk

Lightly brown the flour, and combine with it the butter and milk. Stir to a creamy consistency and set aside.

Heat bacon fat and sauté onions, sweet peppers, and celery. Add crabmeat, stir in cream sauce, and add all other ingredients except paprika. Stir gently, fill crab shells, and sprinkle on paprika. Bake 30 minutes in a 375-degree oven. Yields 4 medium servings.

# Dolphin with Mushroom Sauce

1½ lbs. dolphin fillet
salt and pepper to taste
2 tbsp. butter

MUSHROOM SAUCE
1 can condensed cream of
   mushroom soup
1 cup sour cream
½ tsp. dry mustard
1 tsp. dill weed

Remove skin from fillet. Sprinkle with salt and pepper and place in a greased baking dish. Dot with butter and bake at 375° F. until done (about 10 or 15 minutes).

Combine ingredients for sauce and stir until well blended. About 5 minutes before the fish is done, spread mushroom sauce over top. Heat under broiler until sauce is glazed and slightly browned. Serve immediately to four people.

# Chilled Poached Bass with Cucumber Sauce

3 lbs. bass, snapper, or flounder
   fillets

### Poaching Liquid

| | |
|---|---|
| 1 carrot, cut into rounds | ½ tsp. black pepper |
| 2 onions, sliced | 1 tsp. salt |
| 1 stalk celery, cut into chunks | ½ cup dry white wine |
| 2 bay leaves | 4 tbsp. lemon juice |

In a large, covered saucepan, combine all ingredients with about 1 quart of water. Bring mixture to a boil and simmer 30 minutes at reduced heat. Wrap fish in cheesecloth and lower into liquid, bringing ends of cheesecloth slightly over the edge of the pan. Be sure fish is completely covered. Cover and simmer until done.

Start checking after 5 minutes. When fish flakes easily, remove and set on a platter. Drain before removing cheesecloth. Strain poaching liquid and reserve for courtbouillon or fish stock. Chill fish.

### Cucumber Sauce

| | |
|---|---|
| 3 long, thin cucumbers | 1 cup sour cream |
| 2 tsp. salt | 1 tbsp. chopped fresh dill |
| 1 cup mayonnaise | 1 tsp. lemon juice |

Peel cucumbers, cut in half, and discard seeds. Dice finely and sprinkle with salt. Chill 2 hours, drain, and mix with remaining ingredients. Pour over chilled fish.

Serves four.

# Dolphin with Sesame Seeds

1½ lbs. dolphin fillet, skinned
2 eggs
1 tsp. salt
½ tsp. pepper
½ tsp. dry mustard

3 tbsp. milk
1 tbsp. lemon juice
½ cup flour
1½ cups sesame seeds
¾ cup melted butter

Beat eggs and add milk, salt, pepper, mustard, and lemon juice. Dip fish in mixture and dredge lightly in flour. Dip into egg mixture again and coat well with sesame seeds. Place in baking dish with about half of the butter, pouring the rest over the fish. Bake at 375° F. for about 15 minutes, and then turn, and bake another 10 to 15 minutes.

# Pompano Parmesan

1½ lbs. pompano fillet, skinned
    and cut into four pieces
1 egg, beaten
2 tbsp. milk
4 tbsp. grated Parmesan cheese

½ cup dried bread crumbs
½ tsp. dry mustard
4 tbsp. butter
2 shallots, sliced

Dip fish in egg and milk mixture, and then into a mixture of cheese, mustard, and bread crumbs. Sauté shallots in butter until tender, then remove. Sauté fish in the same pan until golden on both sides (about 5 minutes per side). Place on a platter and pour the pan drippings over it. Serve immediately. Makes enough for four.

# Crabmeat-Stuffed Salmon

1 7- to 10-lb. salmon
1 lemon, halved
1 lb. crabmeat
¼ cup mayonnaise
½ tsp. pepper
½ cup bread crumbs

½ cup finely diced celery
¼ cup chopped chives
¼ cup melted butter
¼ cup chopped parsley
salt to taste
¾ cup dry white wine

Rub inside of salmon with lemon. Combine all ingredients, except salt and wine, and stuff fish. Close with string. Lay fish on a large piece of aluminum foil. Bring up edges of foil and pour wine over fish. Season with salt. Close foil, completely enclosing fish, place in pan, and bake at 375° F. for 1 to 1½ hours. Serves twelve.

# Shrimp-Stuffed Salmon

1 8- to 10-lb. salmon
salt and pepper to taste
Tabasco sauce
soy sauce
1 cup cooked shrimp

2 cups prepared poultry stuffing
lemons
3 tbsp. white wine
4 tbsp. chicken stock

Rub the cavity of the salmon with soy sauce and a few drops of Tabasco. Salt and pepper the outside. Mix stuffing with the shrimp and the juice of ½ lemon; add chicken stock and wine to stuffing until it holds together. Fill cavity of salmon with stuffing.

Place fish on large piece of aluminum foil and seal. Bake about 30 minutes at 350° F. Remove from foil, place stuffing in serving bowl, and garnish fish with lemon wedges. Serves eight to ten diners.

# Trout Stuffed with Shrimp and Clams

6 trout
1 onion, minced
½ lb. sliced mushrooms
olive oil
2 small cans clams
1 cup shrimp, cooked

2 cups sour cream
1 bell pepper, finely diced
¼ tsp. pepper
½ tsp. paprika
½ tsp. allspice
2 lemons

Sauté the onion and mushrooms in oil until tender. Stir in the remaining ingredients except trout and lemons. Stuff each trout with some of the clam-shrimp mixture and place on a piece of oiled aluminum foil. Sprinkle with lemon juice and pour any remaining liquid or stuffing over the fish. Wrap and seal foil and bake at 325° F. for about 30 minutes.

# Bass in Casserole

1 1-lb. bass fillet, cut into 2-in.
  cubes
1 pkg. (10 oz.) frozen chopped
  broccoli
¼ cup cream

1 10½-oz. can cream of shrimp
  soup
½ cup dry white wine
1 cup small shrimp, cooked
3 tbsp. melted butter

Defrost broccoli, drain, and set aside. Combine cream, soup, and wine.

Put the melted butter inside a deep casserole. Place broccoli in the casserole and mix with the butter. Sprinkle shrimp over the broccoli and add the fish cubes. Pour the soup mixture over casserole. Cover and bake at 350° F. for about 20 minutes. Uncover and cook 10 minutes more or until fish is done.

# Striper with Cheese Sauce

*8 striper fillets, ¼ in. thick*

### RICE STUFFING
*1 cup cooked white or wild rice*　　*4 tbsp. chopped mushrooms*
*salt and pepper to taste*　　　　　*3 tbsp. chopped black olives*
*2 tbsp. melted butter*　　　　　　*2 tbsp. dry white wine*

### SWISS CHEESE SAUCE
*2 tbsp. butter*　　　　　　　*½ cup grated Swiss cheese*
*2 tbsp. flour*　　　　　　　　*salt and pepper to taste*
*¾ cup dry white wine*　　　　*1 tsp. dry mustard*
*½ cup cream*

Mix the stuffing ingredients together well. Place 1 heaping tablespoonful in the center of each fillet, fold the ends over stuffing, and secure with toothpicks. Place fillets in a lightly buttered baking dish and add any remaining stuffing between them. Bake, uncovered, at 350° F. for 15 minutes.

On low heat, melt butter in a pan and slowly blend in flour. Add the cream slowly, and then the wine, stirring constantly. Add cheese and stir until completely melted. Remove from heat and add salt, pepper, and mustard. Pour the sauce over the fish and bake for 5 minutes. Serves four.

# Pork-Stuffed Halibut

*1 9- to 10-lb. halibut*　　*4 strips bacon*
*2 lbs. pork sausage*　　　*1 tsp. garlic salt*
*3 onions*　　　　　　　*1 1-lb. can tomatoes with liquid*
*4 lemons*　　　　　　　*1 cup Bordeaux wine*

Wipe fish with a damp paper towel. Stuff cavity with the sausage and 2 coarsely chopped onions. Sew the cavity together and place the fish in a large roasting pan. Slice the remaining onion and 1½ lemons and arrange around the fish. Cover with bacon strips and squeeze the juice of the remaining lemons into the pan. Add wine, garlic salt, and tomatoes and liquid. Bake, uncovered, at 350° F. for about 1½ hours.

## Foiled Bass

4 bass fillets (8 oz. each)
1 cup sour cream
½ cup mayonnaise
2 cups sliced mushrooms, sautéed

2 tbsp. melted butter
salt and pepper to taste
paprika
½ lemon

Combine sour cream, mayonnaise, mushrooms, butter, salt, and pepper. Place each fillet in a piece of aluminum foil and season with a squeeze of lemon. Spoon the sour cream mixture over each, seal, and bake at 350° F. for 20 minutes or until done. Broil uncovered for 1 minute to brown. Sprinkle with paprika; makes four servings.

# Whiting and Brown Gravy

| | |
|---|---|
| *whiting* | *flour* |
| *cracker meal* | *milk* |
| *salt and pepper to taste* | *buttermilk* |

Salt and pepper the whiting and soak in buttermilk for 15 to 30 minutes. Dredge in cracker meal and brown lightly in hot fat. Remove whiting and set aside. Brown enough flour to make a thin paste in the pan drippings. Add milk to make a good, thick gravy. Salt and pepper to taste. Immerse fish and simmer 20 minutes. Serve with rice and salad.

# Vegetables

THIS PART OF THE MEAL may be thought of as ancillary. Not so. Consider anything left on the plate as a drawback to the overall success of the meal. Of course there are times when someone's eyes are bigger than their stomachs, or something else on the "Bill of Fare" far overshadows what is left on the plate. This should not be so with vegetables. They should be considered delectable enough to be a meal within themselves.

You have your favorites, I'm sure, but if these aren't in your armamentarium, they will find a niche in your heart.

# Corn Pudding

| | |
|---|---|
| 3 tbsp. melted butter | 1⅓ cups scalded milk |
| 3 eggs | ¼ small onion, minced |
| 1½ cups whole kernel corn | 1 tbsp. flour |
| 1 tbsp. sugar | 1½ tsp. salt |

Butter a 2-quart casserole. Mix or blend the remaining ingredients until the corn is thoroughly mixed into batter. Pour into the casserole and bake for 70 minutes in a preheated 350-degree oven. Serves six.

# Potato Puffs

| | |
|---|---|
| ½ cup grated American cheese | 1 egg, beaten |
| 2 cups cold mashed potatoes | dry bread crumbs |
| ½ tsp. salt | shortening |
| ⅛ tsp. pepper | |

Combine the first five ingredients, shape into balls, and roll in crumbs. Fry until brown in melted shortening. Yields four to six servings.

# Pennsylvania Red Cabbage

1 medium head red cabbage
½ tsp. caraway seeds
2 tbsp. salad oil or bacon fat
dash pepper

1½ tsp. salt
½ cup brown sugar
2 medium apples, chopped
lemon juice

Chop the cabbage; add to a saucepan along with the caraway seeds.
Mix remaining ingredients, pour over cabbage, and simmer, covered,
for 1 hour. Serves six.

# Fried Cheese

2 tbsp. butter or margarine
2 eggs, slightly beaten
½ cup flour

1 lb. mozzarella cheese
½ cup fine, dry bread crumbs

Dip ¼-inch slices of cheese into flour, then egg, then crumbs, and fry
about 2 minutes on each side in melted butter. When brown, serve to
four to six people.

# Potato Pancakes

3 cups grated raw potatoes
2 eggs
¼ tsp. baking powder

½ small onion, minced
2 tbsp. flour
1 tsp. salt

Combine all ingredients and fry in desired size on a greased griddle or
in butter in a skillet. Makes enough for six.

# Sweet-and-Sour Cabbage

4 cups shredded cabbage
2 tbsp. brown sugar
salt and pepper
2 cloves

4 slices bacon, diced
1 tbsp. flour
⅓ cup vinegar
1 small onion, sliced

Cook cabbage in boiling, salted water for 7 minutes. Fry bacon and set aside. Add sugar and flour to bacon fat; blend. Add ½ cup water to the vinegar and seasonings; cook until thick. Add onion, diced bacon, and cabbage; heat through. Six servings.

# Nice Rice

Place desired amount of rice in a boiler, after washing in cold water three times. Add enough water to reach a level 2 inches over rice. Boil until little holes appear in the rice. Cover, reduce heat, and simmer for 20 minutes.

# Sweet Potato Soufflé

3 cups boiled sweet potato
½ tsp. salt
⅓ stick butter
1 tsp. vanilla

¾ cup sugar
2 eggs
½ cup milk

Mix, place in baking dish, and top with the below mixture.

1 cup light brown sugar
½ cup plain flour

1 cup chopped nuts
⅓ stick butter

Bake 35 minutes at 350° F.

# Hopping John

2 lbs. black-eyed peas
4 cups precooked rice
onions, chopped

1 ham hock
salt and pepper to taste

Boil the dried peas and ham hocks for about 3 hours or until tender. Add rice, salt, and pepper to taste. Sprinkle chopped onions over each serving and serve with fried corn cakes. Serves ten.

# Ham and Rice

3 cups cooked rice
4 tbsp. onion flakes
1 tbsp. ketchup
1 cup hot water

1 cup minced ham
1 tsp. prepared mustard
1 tsp. Tabasco sauce
2 tbsp. cooking oil

Mix in a bowl the rice, ham, seasonings, and water. Transfer the mixture to a pan and allow it to simmer for 15 minutes in hot oil.

# Beans and Rice

¾ cup packaged, precooked rice
¾ cup boiling water
¼ can onion flakes
1 can (2¼ cups) tomatoes
1 tsp. salt
1½ cups cooked or canned meat
  or fish

¼ tsp. salt
2 tbsp. cooking oil
4 tsp. celery salt
½ tsp. sugar
⅛ tsp. Tabasco sauce
1 can French style green beans

Bring the water to a boil in a saucepan. Then add rice and salt. Cover the pan and set it off the heat. Sauté the onion flakes in oil. Add remaining ingredients and cook over medium heat for 20 to 25 minutes. Fluff the rice with a fork and serve the preparation over the rice.

## Juanita's Spanish Rice

6 *slices bacon*
2 *bell peppers, sliced*
3 *tsp. Worcestershire sauce*
2 *tsp. garlic salt*
1 *cup washed, uncooked rice*

2 *large onions, sliced*
5 *cups tomatoes*
*salt and pepper to taste*
1 *lb. ground beef (optional)*

Fry bacon slowly until crisp. Remove from pan and pour off some of the drippings. Brown onions, peppers, and ground beef in the remainder of the fat. Add seasonings and crumbled bacon. Add warmed tomatoes (steamed fresh ones, if possible), stir in the uncooked rice, and cook slowly. Stir often because it sticks easily. If the mixture seems too dry, add more tomatoes or water. Cook until the rice is tender (approximately 45 minutes).

# Squash Casserole

4 lbs. yellow squash
2 carrots
1 small onion, grated
salt and pepper to taste
½ stick butter

1 can cream of mushroom soup
1 pt. sour cream
Pepperidge Farm corn bread
  dressing

Slice and cook squash in salty water; drain. In a mixing bowl add squash, grated carrots, soup, sour cream, onions, salt, and pepper. Melt butter in the bottom of the casserole dish and sprinkle just enough of the dressing to absorb it. Add squash mixture to this and sprinkle more dressing on top, dotting it with butter. Bake for 30 minutes at 350° F.

# Vegetable Kabobs

½ cup butter or margarine
2 tbsp. chopped parsley
⅛ tsp. pepper
3 slices unpared eggplant, cut in
  quarters
1 green pepper, cut in squares
8 cherry tomatoes

3 tbsp. lemon juice
½ tsp. salt
¼ tsp. dried thyme leaf
8 small new potatoes, cooked
1 medium zucchini, cut in
  ½-inch slices
½ tsp. monosodium glutamate

In a small saucepan, melt butter with lemon juice, parsley, salt, pepper, and thyme. Alternate vegetables, except tomatoes, on four 12-inch or eight 6-inch skewers. Place on a grill set 4 inches above charcoal briquets that have reached the light gray stage. Brush vegetables generously with the butter sauce and sprinkle with monosodium glutamate. Grill 10 minutes, turning occasionally and basting frequently with butter sauce. Just before vegetables are tender, add cherry tomatoes to ends of skewers. Continue grilling until all vegetables are tender and tomatoes are heated. Makes four servings.

# Breads and Stuffings

BREADS ARE NOT my forte, but I enjoy them as a very necessary part of a great meal. I don't know why I never pursued the art of baking; maybe it is the sticky quality of the dough I don't like. You might want to leave this part of the meal to your wife or the baker, as either one would do well, I'm sure.

I know you can make these breads, because even I can. I know they are good!

## Spoonbread 1

½ cup cornmeal
2 cups milk
2 tbsp. melted butter or
    margarine

1 tsp. salt
½ tsp. sugar
½ tsp. baking powder
3 eggs, separated

Preheat oven to 375° F. Scald milk, add cornmeal, and cook until thick. Stir in next four ingredients. Add beaten egg yolks. Fold this mixture into egg whites, which have been beaten until stiff. Bake in buttered 1½ quart casserole, uncovered, for 25 to 30 minutes. Serves six.

## Spoonbread 2

¾ cup cornmeal
1 cup milk
2 eggs, well beaten
2 tsp. baking powder

1 cup boiling water
1 tsp. salt
3 tbsp. melted butter

Combine meal, salt, and butter in a mixing bowl. Add water slowly and beat until smooth. Add milk, eggs, and baking powder, mixing well. Turn into a well-greased shallow baking dish and bake at 350° F. for 45 minutes.

# Mexican Corn Bread

1 cup cornmeal
1 cup milk
1 clove garlic, pressed
1 cup cream style corn
2 eggs
1 cup grated sharp cheddar cheese

1 cup chopped onions
½ tsp. salt
½ cup Wesson oil
1 jalapeño, finely chopped
½ tsp. soda

Mix and pour into an adequate baking pan. Bake at 400° F. until browned as desired.

# Corn Bread

2 cups plain meal, sifted
3 tbsp. hot bacon fat
1 egg, beaten
1 cup flour

2 tsp. salt
1 tsp. baking powder
1 cup buttermilk

Place bacon fat in a large iron skillet and slide into a hot oven. Immediately mix the dry ingredients and add milk and egg. Pour hot fat from skillet and mix well with the other ingredients. Pour all into the hot skillet and bake about 20 minutes.

# Cornmeal Dumplings

1 cup plain cornmeal
¼ cup flour

1 tsp. salt
¼ cup water

Mix all ingredients and make a stiff dough. Drop by a tablespoon into boiling pot liquor or turnip greens. Cover and cook for 7 minutes.

# Hush Puppies 1

2 cups yellow cornmeal
¾ cup plain flour
2½ tsp. baking powder

1 tsp. salt
¼ cup finely chopped onions

Mix all of the ingredients except the onions with just enough water to make a thick dough. Add the onions and mix in well. Spoon into deep, hot fat, and fry until golden brown. If dough starts to stick to the spoon, dip spoon into water.

# Hush Puppies 2

½ cup water ground meal
1 egg

½ cup self-rising flour
1 medium onion, finely chopped

Mix the above and blend in beer, buttermilk, or milk until the dough is thick in consistency. Drop into hot fat and remove quickly when golden brown. Hush puppies are best when cooked in hot fish grease.

# Biscuits

3 cups self-rising flour
2 heaping tbsp. Crisco
buttermilk

Place flour in a bowl and cut in Crisco with a fork until well mixed. Pour in enough buttermilk (approximately 3 tablespoons) until the mixture is nearly doughy. Add a little water to attain a doughy consistency. Pinch off a piece the size of a golf ball, roll, flatten, and place in a greased pan. Repeat until the dough is expended. Bake until brown in a preheated 450-degree oven.

# Stovepipe Bread

1 pkg. active dry yeast  
3 ½ cups flour, sifted  
2 eggs  
¼ cup sugar

½ cup milk  
1 tsp. salt  
½ cup salad oil

Add yeast to 1½ cups flour and mix. Combine ½ cup water with the oil, sugar, salt, and milk in a saucepan and warm. Add to flour and yeast mixture and mix until smooth. Add eggs and mix until well blended. Gradually add 1 cup flour, mixing well. Add additional flour to make a soft dough.

Divide batter and place in two well-greased 1-pound coffee cans. Cover with the plastic lids and let them stand in a warm place until dough has risen almost to the top of the can. Remove lids and bake in a preheated oven at 375° F. 30 to 35 minutes, or until browned. Let cool in cans about 10 minutes, and then remove to racks. Yields two small loaves.

# Apple Stuffing for Large Game Birds

3 cups bread crumbs  
1 cup apple juice  
3 cups peeled, cored, and diced  
   apples  
2 onions, finely chopped

2 stalks celery, finely chopped  
6 slices bacon, diced  
6 tbsp. sugar  
1 tbsp. parsley

Fry bacon and remove from skillet. With the exception of the bread crumbs, sauté remaining ingredients in the bacon fat until the apples are almost tender. Add bacon and bread crumbs, mixing well and adding more crumbs if necessary.

# Sweet Corn Bread

1 cup self-rising flour
2 eggs
¼ cup sugar
¼ cup soft bacon drippings

¾ tsp. salt
1 cup milk
1 cup cornmeal, sifted

Mix dry ingredients. Add milk, eggs, and bacon fat. Stir and pour into a greased pan. Bake at 425° F. for 20 to 25 minutes.

# Cracklin' Bread

2 cups cornmeal
1 tbsp. shortening
2½ cups milk
2 tbsp. baking powder
1 cup boiling water

2 eggs
1 tsp. salt
1 cup cracklin' (the crisp residue
    left in a skillet after lard has
    been heated and poured off)

Pour boiling water over cornmeal, add shortening, and allow to cool slightly. Beat the eggs and add to milk and salt. Combine the two mixtures, add baking powder and cracklin', and blend well with a spoon. Pour into a well-greased pan and bake at 400° F. for 25 minutes.

# Cornmeal Hoecakes

2 cups plain cornmeal
1 tsp. baking powder
¾ cup buttermilk

2 tsp. salt
1 tbsp. bacon fat

Mix the dry ingredients. Stir in milk and bacon fat. Pour into a greased, hot skillet and cook for about 5 minutes on each side. Use high heat.

# Dumplings

2 cups all-purpose flour, sifted
3 tsp. baking powder
3 tbsp. shortening

1 tsp. salt
1 cup milk

Sift together dry ingredients and cut in shortening until mixture resembles coarse meal. Add milk and mix with fork until blended. Drop by tablespoon onto meat pieces, not into liquid (this will make dumplings soggy), and cook 10 minutes uncovered, with liquid bubbling. Cover and simmer 10 more minutes.

# Coon Stuffing

3 double handfuls of toasted
    bread crumbs
1 chopped onion, sautéed
2 eggs, beaten

1 cup coon broth
1 tsp. poultry seasoning
1½ tsp. salt

Combine ingredients and mix well.

# Potato Stuffing

3 potatoes, cooked and mashed
1 tbsp. bacon fat
6 slices bacon, fried crisp and
    crumbled
¼ cup cream

1 egg, beaten
salt and pepper to taste
1 medium onion, finely chopped
    and sautéed

Mix all ingredients well.

# Chestnut Stuffing

4 lbs. chestnuts
2 cups bread crumbs
1 cup finely chopped celery

1 cup cream
salt and pepper to taste
½ tsp. grated orange peel

Place chestnuts in water and discard any that float. Cut slits in those remaining and boil for 15 to 20 minutes. Drain, peel off shells, skin, and chop finely or grate.

Sauté celery in bacon fat until tender.

Mix all ingredients well.

# Bread Stuffing

4 cups bread crumbs
2 tbsp. melted butter
1 cup meat broth or bouillon
1 onion, minced

½ cup minced celery
1½ tsp. salt
½ tsp. pepper
1 tbsp. poultry seasoning

Sauté onion and celery. Combine all ingredients and mix well. Chopped giblets may be added or used in gravy.

# Pecan Stuffing for Quail or Pheasant

4 cups bread crumbs
1 large onion, finely chopped
3 stalks celery, finely chopped
1 cup finely chopped pecans

1 cup seedless raisins
salt to taste
2 eggs, beaten
½ cup evaporated milk

Sauté onions and celery in butter until tender. Combine with remaining ingredients.

# Peanut Stuffing 1

2 cups ground salted peanuts
12 slices bread, toasted and diced
½ cup chicken bouillon

Mix peanuts and bread with enough of the bouillon to make a fairly dry dressing.

# Peanut Stuffing 2

3 cups ground or crushed roasted
   peanuts
4 cups dried bread crumbs
3 tsp. melted butter
1 cup finely minced onion

½ tsp. pepper
1 egg, beaten
½ cup chicken bouillon
½ cup white wine

Combine all ingredients.

# Carrot Stuffing

2 carrots, cut into large rounds
½ cup melted butter
1 onion, chopped
2 stalks celery, chopped
salt and pepper to taste

2 cups bread crumbs
1 4½-oz. can black olives,
  chopped
paprika
garlic salt

Parboil carrots until tender.

In a skillet, combine butter, onion, and celery. Season to taste.
Sauté until tender and then add remaining ingredients.

# Fruit and Nut Stuffing

3 Golden Delicious apples, peeled
  and diced
2 tbsp. lemon juice
1 cup cooked white rice
1 cup chopped pecans or walnuts

¼ cup vermouth
¼ tsp. nutmeg
1 tsp. cinnamon
¼ cup brown sugar

Sprinkle apples with lemon juice and then combine with remaining
ingredients.

# Sauces and Marinades

A SAUCE THAT IS PROPERLY chosen can put a zing into a meal that would bring only a smile of approval.

A southern barbecue is an institution that has maintained its popularity for centuries mainly because of well-guarded family barbecue sauce recipes. Many still maintain the axiom that a pig being cooked over coals should be basted periodically with salty water at first and then basted with a simple sauce of vinegar, lemon, and a combination of red and black pepper. The proponents of this process have survived years of praise and notoriety for their prowess.

The choices in this section can enhance practically any meal you wish to prepare.

## Goolsby's Special Barbecue Sauce

¼ box brown sugar  
½ gal. apple cider vinegar  
2 pts. mustard  
1 gal. ketchup  
juice of 2 lemons  

5 tbsp. sugar  
1 cup salt  
½ box black pepper  
⅓ bottle Worcestershire sauce  
½ lb. butter  

Combine ingredients and cook slowly until proper consistency is attained. Use butter rather than margarine; do not refrigerate.

## Quick Hollandaise Sauce

½ cup butter or margarine  
dash cayenne pepper  
2 tbsp. lemon juice  

1 egg  
¼ tsp. salt  

Melt the butter in the top of a double boiler, over hot, but not boiling, water. Add remaining ingredients and mix with a hand mixer until thick and smooth. Remove from heat and serve warm over vegetables. Yields ¾ cup.

# Horseradish Sauce

1 to 2 tbsp. sugar
¼ tsp. salt

1 cup horseradish
¾ cup white vinegar

Combine and mix all ingredients until well blended. Yields 1½ cups.


# Shirley's Sweet-and-Sour Sauce

1 stick margarine
2 tbsp. Worcestershire sauce
1 tbsp. garlic salt
½ cup ketchup
1 tsp. black pepper
2 lemons

2 tbsp. soy sauce
1 tbsp. prepared mustard
⅓ cup tarragon vinegar
½ cup of your favorite jam or
 marmalade

Melt butter and add other ingredients in the order of their listings. This sauce is the coup de grace for pork roast or any chipped barbecue.


# Sweet-and-Sour Basting Sauce

⅓ cup brown sugar
1 tsp. soy sauce
2 tbsp. salad oil
½ clove garlic, crushed
1 tsp. salt
½ cup wine vinegar

⅛ green pepper, minced
2 oz. pimento
6 oz. frozen pineapple juice
 concentrate
strips of green pepper
pineapple chunks

Blend the first nine ingredients until smooth. Brush on meat while it broils, barbecues, or roasts. Garnish with pepper strips and pineapple. Yields 1 cup.

# French Style Basting Sauce

¼ cup French dressing
1 tbsp. grated onion
dash pepper

1 tbsp. lemon juice
2 tsp. salt

Combine ingredients.

# Barbecue Sauce 1

⅓ cup salad oil
2 tbsp. soy sauce
14 oz. ketchup
1 tbsp. brown sugar

½ cup consommé, undiluted
½ tsp. salt
¼ cup wine vinegar
dash garlic powder

Combine all ingredients and mix well. Heat and use as a basting sauce while barbecueing. Yields 2½ cups.

# Barbecue Sauce 2

2¼ cups ketchup
¾ tsp. cayenne pepper
½ cup tarragon vinegar
1 cup brown sugar
1 tbsp. finely minced onion

2½ tbsp. Worcestershire sauce
¾ tsp. chili powder
½ cup salt pork liquor
6 cloves garlic, pressed
1 tbsp. black pepper

Combine all ingredients in a saucepan. Bring to a boil and then simmer. Salt pork liquor is made by boiling 2 thick strips of salt pork in 1½ cups of water for 10 minutes. Smoked bacon may be used.

# Oriental Meat Sauce

1 tbsp. ginger

3 tbsp. vinegar

3 tbsp. water

3 tbsp. brown sugar

2½ tbsp. soy sauce

2 pressed garlic buttons

3 tbsp. oil

3 tbsp. ketchup

1 tbsp. dry mustard

1 tbsp. cornstarch

Simmer and stir until slightly viscous. Apply to fowl or pork with great results.

# Smoky Butter Basting Sauce

½ cup butter or fat, melted

1 tbsp. chopped parsley

2 tsp. salt

2 tbsp. lemon juice

1 tbsp. hickory smoke liquid

dash pepper

Combine ingredients.

# Lemon Butter Basting Sauce

½ cup butter or fat, melted

2 tsp. salt

¼ cup lemon juice

½ tsp. Worcestershire sauce

Combine ingredients.

# Roux

The basis of many dishes is the roux. This is a gravy made by slowly browning flour in melted shortening or butter. Use approximately equal amounts of butter and flour. After this mixture reaches a dark brown color, gradually add hot water or stock and stir constantly. Add any other desired ingredients, herbs, and spices.

# Peach Sauce

*2½ cups fresh sliced peaches*
*2 tbsp. butter*
*pepper to taste*

*1 tbsp. grated orange peel*
*2 cups red wine*
*4 to 6 duck livers*

Rub peaches through a ricer or colander. Add the next four ingredients and boil. Put livers through ricer or colander and add to sauce with some duck meat pan drippings. Lower heat and simmer for about 20 minutes.

Applesauce may be used instead of peaches.

# Game Marinades

GAME MARINADE 1
*2 cups red wine*
*2 tbsp. Worcestershire sauce*
*1 tbsp. meat tenderizer*
*3 tbsp. soy sauce*
*2 bay leaves*
*4 beef bouillon cubes*

*4 cloves garlic, crushed*
*1 cup vinegar*
*1 tbsp. tarragon*
*juice of 1 lemon*
*1 onion, sliced*

## GAME MARINADE 2

2 cups claret
2 cups vinegar
1 tbsp. Worcestershire sauce

1 bay leaf
2 whole cloves
dash salt

## GAME MARINADE 3

2 cups dry white wine
2 cups tarragon vinegar
1 bell pepper, chopped
1 onion, sliced

1 tbsp. black pepper
3 bay leaves
6 whole cloves

## GAME MARINADE 4

1 cup dry white wine
2 tbsp. tarragon vinegar

2 cloves garlic, pressed
2 tbsp. soy sauce

## GAME MARINADE 5

½ cup tarragon vinegar
½ cup water
juice of 1 lemon
½ tsp. black pepper
2 tsp. salt

1 bay leaf
1 tsp. chili powder
1 clove garlic, crushed
2 onions, sliced

## GAME MARINADE 6

1 bottle dry white wine
½ cup oil
1 cup vinegar
1 tsp. salt
½ tsp. black pepper

½ tsp. tarragon, thyme, or
    rosemary
2 sprigs parsley, chopped
4 shallots, chopped
2 carrots, sliced

# Relishes and Preserves

# Zucchini Relish

10 cups ground zucchini
4 cups ground onions
5 tbsp. salt
2¼ cups white vinegar
4½ cups sugar
1 tbsp. nutmeg
1 tbsp. turmeric

1 tbsp. dry mustard
1 tbsp. cornstarch
½ tsp. pepper
2 tsp. celery salt
1 sweet green pepper, chopped
1 red pepper, chopped

Place the first three ingredients in a large bowl and mix well. Let stand overnight. Drain and rinse in cold water. Drain again and place in a large kettle with remaining ingredients. Bring to a boil and simmer, uncovered, stirring occasionally, for 30 minutes. Pour into hot sterilized jars and seal. Process 5 minutes.

# Pear Relish

4 qts. peeled, cored, and
   quartered pears
6 green peppers, meat only
1 qt. chopped onions
¼ tsp. cayenne pepper
1 pt. dill pickles, drained

1 cup salt
2 cups sugar
1½ tbsp. flour
1 tsp. turmeric
2 tbsp. dry mustard
1 qt. white vinegar

Run the first five ingredients through a medium-cut meat grinder. Add salt and refrigerate overnight. Drain the mixture, wash once in cold water, and drain again.

In a big kettle combine all of the remaining ingredients; stir well and boil for 5 minutes. Add the pear mixture, continue to stir, and bring the kettle to a boil again. Boil and stir for 5 more minutes.

Pack the mixture in eight hot sterilized pint jars and seal. Process for 20 minutes.

# Red Cabbage Relish

4 cups finely chopped red cabbage
1 small green pepper, chopped
   finely
1 medium onion, minced
1 tbsp. salt

½ tsp. dry mustard
⅛ tsp. white pepper
⅓ cup sugar
1 cup cider vinegar

Combine vegetables in a mixing bowl, sprinkle with salt, and let stand for 1 hour. Add the remaining ingredients and mix well. Chill for 1 hour. May be stored in refrigerator while covered. Makes 1 quart.

# Chow Chow 1

1 peck green tomatoes
4 green bell peppers
6 large onions
1 tsp. turmeric
6 heads cabbage

4 red bell peppers
1 tbsp. pickling spice
4 cups sugar
1 qt. vinegar

Coarsely grind all but the sugar and vinegar and let stand overnight. Drain off the liquid. Add the sugar and vinegar and cook for 15 minutes. Place in sterilized jars and seal.

# Chow Chow 2

3 lbs. green tomatoes
3 large onions
3 green bell peppers
6 firm ripe apples
3 red bell peppers
3 cups white vinegar

2 cups sugar
2 tbsp. pickling spices
1 tbsp. dry mustard
1 tbsp. salt
1 tsp. celery seed

Combine the tomatoes, onions, apples, and bell peppers. Run through a medium grinder and place in a large kettle. Add the remaining ingredients, mix well, and boil. Simmer for 15 minutes, stirring occasionally. Pour into sterilized jars, seal, and process for 5 minutes.

## Sweet Pepper Relish

12 red sweet peppers, finely
   chopped
12 medium onions, finely
   chopped
4 tbsp. salt

12 green sweet peppers, finely
   chopped
2 cups vinegar
2 cups sugar

Combine the peppers and onions, cover with boiling water, and let stand for 5 minutes. Drain. Mix vinegar and sugar and bring to a boil. Add peppers and onions and simmer for 30 minutes. Place in sterilized jars and seal.

    Gelatin may be added to make sweet pepper jelly.

## Chili Relish

2 qts. chopped, peeled tomatoes
1 cup chopped green onions
½ cup coarsely ground sweet red
   pepper
½ cup coarsely ground green
   pepper
½ tsp. cinnamon

1 cup sugar
1½ tsp. salt
1½ tsp. white mustard seed
1 tsp. crushed and dried red
   pepper
1¼ cups white sugar

Combine all ingredients in a large kettle, bring to a boil, and simmer for 3 hours, stirring frequently. Pour into sterilized ½-pint jars; seal. Process 5 minutes.

# Corn Relish

10 large ears of corn, cut in
   niblets from cob
2 large onions, chopped
3 sweet red peppers, chopped
3 green peppers, chopped
½ medium head of cabbage,
   chopped

2 cups sugar
1 tbsp. dry mustard
1 tbsp. celery seed
1 tbsp. salt
1 tbsp. turmeric
2½ cups vinegar

Combine all ingredients and ½ cup water in a large kettle, bring to a
boil, and simmer, uncovered, stirring occasionally, for 25 minutes.
Place into five hot sterilized pint jars and seal. Process 5 minutes.

# Pickled Okra

2 lbs. fresh tender okra
10 cloves garlic
6 tbsp. salt

5 pods hot red or hot green pepper
3 cups vinegar
1 tbsp. mustard seed

Wash okra and pack in jars. Distribute the garlic and pepper to the jars.
Add 1 cup water to the remaining ingredients and bring to a boil. Pour
into jars to within ½ inch of the top and seal.

# Green Tomato Pickles

4 qts. thinly sliced green tomatoes
⅓ cup salt
1 tsp. whole allspice
1 tsp. celery seed
1 lemon, thinly sliced

1 qt. thinly sliced onions
3 cups vinegar
3 cups brown sugar (packed)
1 tbsp. black peppercorns
⅛ tsp. cayenne

Place tomatoes and onions in a large bowl and sprinkle with salt. Cover and let stand overnight. Drain.

Bring the remaining ingredients to a boil. Add the tomatoes and onions and boil; then simmer, stirring several times for about 10 minutes. Pour into sterilized jars and process for 5 minutes.

## Sweet Cauliflower Pickles

2 heads cauliflower, separated
   into florets
2 green peppers (strips)
1 qt. vinegar
½ cup light corn syrup
1 tbsp. celery seed
¼ tsp. turmeric

2 sweet red peppers (strips)
1 qt. onion wedges
2 cups sugar
1 tbsp. mustard
1 tsp. whole cloves
2 tbsp. salt

Cook cauliflower in a small amount of unsalted water for 5 minutes. Drain. Combine remaining ingredients and bring to a boil. Add cauliflower and bring to a boil again. Drain and pack into sterilized jars. Process for 5 minutes.

## Fresh Kosher Style Pickles

36 3- to 4-inch-long cucumbers
3 cups vinegar
6 tbsp. salt

fresh or dried dill
garlic
mustard seed

Wash cucumbers. Mix vinegar, 3 cups water, and salt and bring to a boil. Place a generous layer of dill and ¾ tsp. mustard seed in bottom of each quart jar. Pack in cucumbers to half fill each jar. Place in another layer of dill and complete filling jars. Fill to within ½ inch of top with boiling brine. Tightly cap jars and process for 15 minutes.

# Sliced Cucumber Pickles

pickling cucumbers
½ tsp. mustard seed
1 tsp. mixed pickling spice
2 large onions, sliced

2 cups vinegar
1 cup sugar
salt

Soak cucumbers in cold water overnight. Drain. Slice ¼ inch thick with a serrated vegetable cutter. Bring all other ingredients except salt and onions to a boil with 1 cup water. Add cucumbers and bring to boil again for 3 minutes or until green appearance is gone from cucumbers. Pack cucumbers into jars, and add 1 tsp. salt and a few onion slices to each jar. Bring the juice to a boil and pour over pickles. Seal and process for 5 minutes.

# Tomato Jam

2¼ lbs. ripe tomatoes
¼ cup lemon juice
1 bottle fruit pectin

1½ tsp. grated lemon rind
6 cups sugar

Scald, peel, and chop tomatoes. Bring to a boil and simmer for 10 minutes. Place 3 cups in a saucepan, add all ingredients except pectin, and mix. Boil hard for 1 minute while stirring. Remove from heat and add pectin. Skim off foam, stir, and repeat. Ladle into hot sterilized jars and pour on a ⅛-inch layer of hot paraffin.

# Peach and Melon Conserve

2 cups diced cantaloupe
3 cups sugar
1 cup chopped walnuts

2 cups diced peaches
juice and grated rind of 2 lemons

Mix all ingredients except nuts in a saucepan. Place over low heat and bring to a boil. Simmer, occasionally stirring, for 1¼ hours. Add nuts and pour immediately into hot sterilized jars.

# Red Pepper Preserves

12 sweet red peppers
2 cups vinegar

1 tbsp. salt
3 cups sugar

Grind peppers with a medium grinder. Add salt and let stand over-night. Drain well and place in a kettle with the vinegar and sugar. Cook 45 minutes, uncovered, stirring occasionally. Pour into sterilized jars, seal, and process 5 minutes.

# Fruit Marmalade

1 cantaloupe
fresh peaches
1 pkg. powdered pectin

1 15-oz. can crushed pineapple
2 tbsp. fresh lemon juice
8 cups sugar

Run cantaloupe and pineapple through a coarse food grinder. Drain off juice. Grind peaches, drain, and add to fruits to make 6 cups. Place in a kettle with lemon juice and pectin and bring to a boil while stirring. Add sugar and bring to a hard boil, stirring. Boil for 8 minutes more, pour into sterilized jars, and seal.

# Strawberry Jam

2 qts. strawberries  
7 cups sugar

¼ cup lemon juice  
½ bottle fruit pectin

Crush the berries well and place 3¾ cups into a saucepan. Add lemon juice and sugar and mix well. Place over high heat and boil hard for 1 minute. Remove from heat and add pectin. Skim off foam; stir and skim several times. Ladle into sterilized glasses and cover at once with a ⅛-inch layer of hot paraffin.

# Peach Jam

3 lbs. ripe peaches  
7½ cups sugar

¼ cup lemon juice  
½ bottle fruit pectin

Grind peeled peaches very finely and measure 4 cups into a saucepan. Stir in lemon juice and sugar. Boil hard for 1 minute while stirring. Remove from heat and stir in pectin. Skim off foam, stir, and repeat. Pour into hot sterilized jars and cover with ⅛ inch hot paraffin.

# Strawberry Jelly

2½ qts. ripe strawberries  
7½ cups sugar

¼ cup lemon juice  
1 bottle fruit pectin

Crush berries and strain juice through a jelly cloth. Place 3¾ cups in a saucepan. Add lemon juice and sugar and mix well. Place over high heat and bring to a boil while stirring. Stir in pectin and boil hard while stirring for 1 minute. Remove from heat, skim off broth and pour into sterilized jelly glasses. Immediately cover with ⅛ inch hot paraffin.

# Hot Pepper Jelly

1 cup chopped bell pepper          1⅓ cups vinegar
6½ cups sugar                      1 bottle Certo
10 hot red peppers

Mix together and bring to a boil. Stir and boil for 3 minutes. Remove from heat and add 1 bottle Certo. Ladle into glasses and pour on ⅛ inch hot paraffin.

# Desserts

# Moist Chocolate Pound Cake

4 eggs
2 cups sugar
1 cup butter or Crisco
1 4-oz. bar German sweet
   chocolate, melted

2 tsp. salt
3 cups flour
½ tsp. soda
1 cup buttermilk

Cream the butter and sugar. Add the eggs one at a time, mixing well after each. Add the vanilla and chocolate; blend. Sift dry ingredients together and add alternately with buttermilk to the sugar mixture. Pour batter into a lightly greased 10-inch tube pan. Bake at 300° F. for 1½ hours. When done, let stand 10 minutes in pan, then remove and cool.

# Chocolate Pie

1 large carton Cool Whip
1 frozen pie shell

1 6½-oz. bar unsweetened
   chocolate

Melt chocolate and fold in Cool Whip. Pour into pie shell, sprinkle with nuts, and refrigerate. Serve when cool and firm.

# Lemon Pie

1 large carton of Cool Whip
1 6-oz. can frozen lemonade

½ can sweetened condensed milk
1 frozen pie shell

Combine the first three ingredients well and pour into the pie shell. Refrigerate until firm and serve.

# One-Egg Cake

1½ cups sifted cake flour (or 3
   tbsp. less of all-purpose flour)
½ tsp. salt
¾ cup granulated sugar
2 tsp. baking powder

½ cup milk
⅓ cup soft shortening
1 tsp. vanilla (or 1 tbsp. grated
   lemon or orange rind)
1 egg

Preheat oven to 375° F. Grease and flour an 8-inch-square pan. Sift together into a large bowl the flour, salt, sugar, and baking powder. Add the next three ingredients and mix well. Add the egg and beat again. Bake in pan for about 25 minutes or until done. Cool and ice as desired. Serves nine.

# Caramel Frosting

⅔ cup evaporated milk
⅔ stick margarine
2 cups sugar

⅛ tsp. salt
1 tsp. vanilla

Melt ¼ cup of sugar in pan; add ¼ cup hot water. Stir and cook until completely smooth. Combine salt, milk, margarine, and remaining sugar in another pan. Pour hot syrup into this mixture and place over high heat. Stir constantly until it boils. This should be about 236° F. on a candy thermometer. Cool to 140° F., add 1 tsp. vanilla, beat, and spread at once. Will frost two 8-inch layers.

# Baked Apples

6 apples, cored
6 tsp. butter

12 tbsp. brown sugar
cinnamon

Put butter, brown sugar, and a dash of cinnamon in the center of each apple. Wrap in foil and cook on a grill or in a 350-degree oven until soft. You may serve with whipped cream topping. Serves six.

# Almond Coffee Cookies

½ cup margarine
1 cup packed brown sugar
1 egg
1 tbsp. instant coffee

1 tsp. vanilla
3 cups self-rising flour
2 tbsp. sherry
½ cup roasted, diced almonds

Cream margarine and sugar. Add egg and beat well; add vanilla and coffee, mixing well. Mix in sherry and almonds. Shape dough into 2 rolls about 1½ inches in diameter. Wrap in foil or plastic wrap and chill 2 to 3 hours. Cut into thin slices and arrange on a lightly greased cookie sheet. Turn oven to 350° F. as cookies are put in. Bake about 10 minutes or until lightly browned. Baking time may need to be reduced to 8 minutes if more sheets of cookies are cooked. Makes 4 to 5 dozen.

# Pecan Pie

1 unbaked 9-inch pie crust
⅛ tsp. salt
¾ cup sugar
1 tbsp. flour
1 tsp. vanilla

2 tbsp. melted butter
1 cup dark corn syrup
1 cup pecan halves
2 eggs, beaten

Preheat oven to 400° F. Mix salt, sugar, flour, vanilla, butter, corn syrup, and eggs until well blended. Add pecans and pour into the pie shell. Bake for 15 minutes, reduce heat to 350° and bake 30 to 35 minutes more, until set. Cool before serving. Serves eight.

# Indian Meal Pudding

¾ cup cornmeal
3 qts. milk
6 cups finely cut apples

3 tsp. salt
3 tsp. ground ginger
1½ cups molasses

Scald milk, add cornmeal, and cook for 30 minutes. Add the remaining ingredients and pour into a buttered baking dish. Bake at 350° F. for 1 hour, stirring occasionally. Twelve servings.

# Peach Ice Cream

1 large can evaporated milk
1 can condensed milk
2 qts. scalded homogenized milk

1½ cups sugar
2 tbsp. vanilla
6 large blended peaches

Mix canned milk, sugar, and vanilla. Add scalded milk and cool in refrigerator until ready to put into churn. Churn until half-frozen, add peaches, and finish churning.

# Baked Bananas

6 bananas, peeled
miniature marshmallows
chocolate chips (or candy bar)

Cut a V-shaped groove from end to end in each banana. Fill with marshmallows and chocolate. Wrap in foil and bake in a 400-degree oven for about 10 minutes. Six servings.

# Trifle

sponge cake
jam or jelly

small amount of cooking sherry
canned or prepared pudding

Cut cake into layers. Place layers in a bowl or pan with your choice of
jam or jelly between each layer. Pour cooking sherry over this and top
with pudding. Chill before serving.

# Appendix

# Tips on Hunting White-tailed Deer

A FULL DISCOURSE on this subject would require a book covering each facet of hunting methods in the whitetail's various habitats. However, for the novice deer hunter, these thoughts should be helpful and should gain top priority:

1. You are hunting one of North America's wiliest large game animals. It has been debated heatedly which of its senses is most acute: visual, olfactory, or auditory. My guess is that the sense of smell is the least sharp, hearing next, and vision the sharpest sense, although it is possible that the white-tailed deer is color-blind. Awareness of all three is a must.

2. Know your weapon and practice with it. Learn, by asking, what caliber gun is best suited for your area and the ballistics that will do more for helping your average. Shoot enough rounds to gain confidence in your proficiency. Firing at a deer is a tough way to learn your gun, considering the fact that a target will remain still until you are ready to put some meat on the table; not so with whitetail.

All of this is important, but doesn't nearly approach the importance of SAFETY! One bad mistake with a gun and not only will you never enjoy your venison, but hardly anything else in life. Be safe, be sure, and be aware.

3. If possible, scout your hunting area several times before the season starts. This is quite a necessary function unless you hunt as a guest of someone who has done this for you. Several considerations to make when scouting are topography, game trails, buck signs, current food supply, cover, visibility, and proximity of other hunters.

4. Feeding habits vary in different areas, dependent on the phase of the season. For instance, the season in Jasper County, Georgia, opens for guns in early November. Usually the food in early October abounds, remaining from summer greenery, as we have not usually had our first frost.

The first acorns to fall are not palatable because they are mostly wormy. The later acorns are readily eaten; thus a stand located in an oak grove is most desirable. Later in the year, after a killing frost, the choice browse is evergreens such as honeysuckle. Pine thickets supply bedding places and an abundance of mushrooms. As hunting pressure increases, look to heavy cover for your best results.

Most of us aren't lucky enough to hunt around old homesteads, but don't overlook apple orchards, sawdust piles, or rock outcroppings, as I feel the deer like landmarks such as these.

5. Patience pays off. Maintain yours and your chance for success is increased. This is a tough fight sometimes, but the greatest problem a hunting lodge operator has is the hunter who has trouble handling his disappointments at not scoring. I'm sure Frank Buck, Jason Lucas, Jimmy Jack John, and even Tarzan have experienced this problem before. I know I have, but an individual who desires to excel uses this as a whetstone for the future rather than an anchor of the past.

6. Did you ever notice how a cat's eyes, a deer's eyes, and a night hawk's eyes shine like lights when seen in your auto's headlights? Did you ever wonder why? Perhaps it's because they are nocturnal beings, as are some people. If you could see in the dark and it was legal, I'd say you would kill tenfold more deer. That is when they move, feed, water, and play most often. This accounts for the fact that most scores are made near dusk or dawn.

7. Stalking is a tactic of the very experienced and patient hunter. If you can move like a breeze, but slower and quieter; blend like smoke, but quicker and with no essence; and persevere like Joan of Arc, then maybe you'll gain a smile for your face and a right to puff out your chest. Just maybe.

8. To help overcome the senses of sight and smell that the quarry possesses, I suggest building a tree stand. Build it sturdy, with comfort in mind, because if it is comfortable, you can sit in it for a long period of time without becoming cramped or having to move about. The whitetail has tremendous peripheral vision and can detect a small movement—then quickly redistribute the leaves on the forest floor.

Tradition dictates that the liver and heart of the opening day kills be cooked for the evening meal. By utilizing the above information you may be the provider of this meal.

The white-tailed deer is an exceptional animal and has the capability to escape unscathed and to make exceptions of all the beforementioned rules except one. The big number Two, SAFETY!

# Cleaning and Dressing Game

## Venison

Field dressing and proper handling is a must. There are as many varied procedures for field dressing and cutting venison as there are for cooking it. The following is our way, which has served us well. If you prefer another, then I suggest you use the most comfortable way for you. You will need this equipment to field dress and cut up your venison:

     sharp knife
     cheesecloth
     2 12-in. strings
     12-ft. length of ¼-in. rope
     meat saw
     plastic bag for liver, heart, and kidneys
     hunting license

Before reaching your downed buck, determine carefully if it is really a kill, or you might lose your venison and your composure.

Some bucks have escaped while having their picture taken or while awaiting the coup de grace.

Place the deer's head uphill and cut the scent glands from the inside of the lower hind legs (WIPE KNIFE WELL). These glands are covered by a somewhat darker patch of long hair and are functional in the mate selection process during the rutting season. Next, remove the exterior genitalia. Cut a swath of fur in a perimeter about three inches around the organs and skin it out, removing the genitalia. Bear in mind that body wastes must not touch the meat. Wipe your knife well after this procedure.

Now remove the viscera. Through the skinned out place, insert your knife tip only to the point of the body cavity; any deeper penetration might puncture the intestines and make the dressing out more distasteful.

If you're right handed, insert and spread your left index and middle finger into the incision, pointing toward the head. Place the knife tip between the fingers and slide both the knife and the left hand toward the head, with the two inserted fingers pushing the intestines away from the path of the knife blade. Proceed carefully until you reach the breastbone. It is no longer necessary to use great care since you've passed the diaphragm and are in the lung and heart area. Do not cut beyond the cowlick on the chest if you plan to shoulder-mount your trophy.

Starting in the neck area, cut away restraining tissues so you can pull out all the entrails and organs. Cut out the diaphragm and procede toward the tail. Save the heart, liver (venison liver has no gallbladder attached), and kidneys.

Cut out the colon and bladder by circling the anus from the exterior. Again, be careful not to cut the bladder. The colon and bladder should be tied off with two strings to prevent a leak. At this point tie off the alimentary tube.

Roll your deer over and lift up its head to allow the blood to drain from the body cavity. Cut a stick approximately 1 inch in diameter and about 1½ feet long. Use it to prop open the chest cavity, allowing the meat to cool more quickly. Be sure to cut off the windpipe as far up as possible since it spoils easily.

Back at camp you may skin your buck out with ease, but be sure not to get hair, leaves, or dirt on freshly skinned venison; small matter adheres tenaciously to the meat. See a taxidermist for care of the hide for tanning and of the legs for use as gun racks.

Allow the deer to hang until it is adequately cooled. To insure that flies do not light on the meat, a cheesecloth draping works nicely, as does a liberal sprinkling of black pepper. One medium deer, properly dressed, will supply a family with delicious meat for about a month, cooked daily from freezer or smokehouse storage.

The full, uncut venison should be cured at about 36° Fahrenheit for approximately two weeks with the hide off (this prevents tainting of the meat by the hair, although it will dry out considerably on the exterior). The kidneys, heart, and liver are suitable for eating immediately after the kill, but the other meat can upset your stomach if not cured first.

If it is impossible to hang your deer this long, it can be cut up after it has cooled without losing too much of its taste. The method is as follows: Cut off each shoulder, starting under the armpits, while pulling the front leg outward. Proceed cutting through the shoulder blade.

Make a cut line with the knife from the bottom of the rib line to the collar bone area and saw off the ribs to save for barbecue. They have some tallow, but can be prepared to taste super.

Cut off and discard the brisket area; I have not found a decent way to prepare it. If you discover one let me know!

Saw the backbone in half to separate the hind legs (hams) from the rest of the body, leaving the loin intact. The hams can be roasted whole or cut up into roasts, and the round steaks can be made into country style steaks and Swiss steaks. After curing the meat (if possible), the hams can be frozen and then easily cut with a meat band saw in uniformly thick pieces (½ inch), wrapped, labeled, and stored in your freezer.

Saw the neck off where the loin ends and remove the meat from the bone. It can be used in stews or venison burgers.

Next is the step that provides the best cut of venison—the loin. Some hunters cut these into chops (as with pork chops), but I prefer the boneless loin. First, place the backbone section on a table, dorsal side up. With a sharp boning knife, cut the loin from the dorsal spinous process by cutting downward alongside the spinous process to the lateral bone, always working with fingers downward, out, and away from the bone. Cut forward to the end in this fashion. With a little help from the knife, and careful attention to the procedure, the full loin can be easily removed.

Now roll the backbone over and separate the smaller lower loin, or backstrap, which is at least as delicious. Small bits of lean meat adhering to the bone may be used as stew or ground meat.

Freeze the loins, securely wrapped and airtight. When freezing the cut-up venison, try to wrap it in airtight packages, marking each package according to the number of people it will feed and signifying the cut of meat. Each medium loin will feed four hearty diners or six less ravenously hungry people.

Proper preparation of the meat will ensure that the venison will not remain stored in the freezer too long, and will gain you much respect from all who try your cooking—even your in-laws.

## Venison Cuts and Cooking

ROASTING: shoulder, flat, and round cut roasts
BROILING: steaks and chops
GRILLING: steaks, chops, and liver
BRAISING: shoulder, neck, breast, heart, and liver
PAN BROILING: steaks and chops
STEWING: shanks, shoulder, neck, and non-fatty scraps
HAMBURGER: all lean meat unused in another fashion

## Loving Care for your Pheasant

Pheasants are relatively low in fat, so exogenous fat must be added when cooking to prevent dryness. This can be averted by cooking in a moist fashion. Perhaps this explains the proposition that "pheasant under glass" maintains this texture. In any event, pheasant is as delicious a bird on the table as it is exotic in the field.

## Dressing the Armadillo

Using a sharp knife, cut the meat on the underside of the tail and head away from the shell, as far as can be reached. Pull the head away from the shell and simultaneously cut the meat from the shell. The carcass should come away from the shell cleanly. Use shears to cut off the head and feet. Cut through the belly muscle and use shears to cut through pelvic and breast bones. Holding the carcass by the tail, cut or pull out all entrails. Remove all sweat glands and fat. Cut off tail. Wash and cook your favorite way.

# Cooking Preparation for Duck and Goose
## Strong Ducks (diving and fish eating)

Soak the birds overnight in a mixture of 2 tablespoons salt, 1 table-spoon soda, and 1 quart water. The heretofore gamey taste can be diminished even more by using a simple stuffing such as the following, which is discarded after cooking: Celery, onion, and whole orange (all chopped); celery tops, onion, apple, and parsley (all chopped). Your choice of a stuffing may also be used.

# Hunter's Kitchen and Wifemanship

For me, a complete kitchen is a must in the preparation of food. Consider that much of your game must be trimmed and readied for cooking, whereas most store-bought food is already prepared for cooking or warming.

Aside from the usual pots, pans, and utensils your live-in cook uses, these items would be advisable:

| | |
|---|---|
| *Meat saw* | *Ice cracker* |
| *Long, curved meat slicing knife* | *Shrimp peeler and deveiner* |
| *Boning knife* | *Full spice and herb rack* |
| *Knife sharpener* | *Meat tenderizer* |
| *Food chopper* | *Rolling pin* |
| *Vegetable slicer* | *Sifter* |
| *Heavy colander* | *Garlic press* |
| *Meat grinder* | *Meat syringe* |
| *Freezer containers* | |

Men in general, and hunters in particular, can and do spoil a kitchen's appearance much to the chagrin of the wife. It has been suggested, however, that if you clean the kitchen after dinner two or three times with a display of diminishing desire, you can soon completely escape this less than pleasant duty.

The quality of your food can be a great lever for praise from the most hard-boiled spouse. Keep in mind that the food you prepare will have a direct effect on her willingness to have you go hunting next time. It will provide her with a more rational outlook as to the emotional and therapeutic value of a restful, tension-relieving, mind-freeing, and fruitful hunt. A gleeful, amorous return punctuated with sincere statements of how great it is to be home and what a genteel atmosphere prevailed at the camp will insure a return trip soon.

A nice kitchen gift such as a food chopper, meat grinder, vegetable slicer, sheer negligee, chef's knife, cheese slicer, chocolate covered cherries (if she likes them), long curved meat knife, or a bottle of "Sinful Soul" perfume will also temper the coldest heart.

When you finish your meal, a dishwasher will allow you to enjoy a good cigar and after dinner conversation—or whatever. So much for skimming the surface of wifemanship.

# Weights and Measures

Having never measured anything, I'm forced to speak in generalities.

| | |
|---|---|
| 1 pinch | = a darn little bit |
| 1 teaspoon | = a little bit |
| 1 tablespoon | = a good bit |
| 1 cup | = 16 good bits |
| 4 cups | = a heap |
| 1 quart | = another heap |
| 1 gallon | = 4 heaps |
| 1 peck | = 8 heaps |
| 1 bushel | = too darn much |

Now here's a table for the more exacting:

| | |
|---|---|
| 1 dash | = 2-3 drops |
| 3 teaspoons | = 1 tablespoon |
| 16 tablespoons | = 1 cup |
| 1 cup | = 8 fluid ounces |
| 2 cups | = 1 pint |
| 4 cups | = 1 quart |
| 4 quarts | = 1 gallon |
| 8 quarts | = 1 peck |
| 4 pecks | = 1 bushel |

# Index